P9-DHN-124

You've never read a book like this one: frankly self-deprecating, boldly complex, intense, joyfully honest, devastatingly beautiful, heartbreakingly funny. *What Falls from the Sky* is about so much more than one woman's year without the Internet; it's about marriage and choices, faith and rest, community and family, grief and hope, food and dirt—all the things that make our lives worth living. It is impossible to live an unexamined life with Esther as your friend. She is completely herself, and so her story sings of freedom within the silence and even within the noise.

   —*Sarah Bessey,* author of *Jesus Feminist* and *Out of Sorts:*
      Making Peace with an Evolving Faith

I tore through this book like the pages were on fire. Esther Emery's courageous, gritty, and self-aware experiment with fasting from the Internet is nothing less than a freedom song. This book is a must-read for anyone who has struggled with finding connection and meaning in a world where communication is reduced to texts, pixels, and emojis. Esther's story will provide fresh perspective and inspiration.

   —*Elizabeth Esther,* author of *Girl at the End of the World*
      and *Spiritual Sobriety*

Esther Emery makes me believe in a different kind of world: where the table, not the screen, has primacy of place; where people change; where silence unfurls—and God still speaks. I'm grateful for that world and the Christ who makes it possible.

   —*Jen Pollock Michel,* author of *Teach Us to Want:*
      Longing, Ambition, and the Life of Faith; and *Keeping Place:*
      Reflections on the Meaning of Home

What Falls from the Sky is a keenly observed exploration of life on the other side of blogs, Twitter, and Facebook. Emery's rich self-awareness and observation of the world harmonize masterfully, and this debut is rich with wit, irony, and grace. A year richly lived, this is a book to be savored.

—*Preston Yancey,* author of *Out of the House of Bread:*
Satisfying Your Hunger for God with the Spiritual Disciplines

What started for Esther as an experiment of whittling down turned into a journey of abundance. I was riveted from the first page, and when I reached the last, I felt I had gained a new friend. Profound and gentle, compelling and engaging, Esther's story will spur you on to love and live better.

—*Amy Boucher Pye,* author of *Finding Myself in Britain*

In this remarkable debut, Esther puts hard stop to the chaos of the Internet and lets the waters settle enough to peer into her own soul. And by showing us, unflinchingly, what she finds there, she gives us the courage to get quiet, get attentive, and listen to our own lives.

—*Addie Zierman,* author of *When We Were on Fire*
and *Night Driving*

Esther Emery's *What Falls from the Sky* is a joyful pilgrimage into the heart of what matters in a complex and connected world. With wit and wisdom, she takes us on a wholehearted journey of an embodied faith: a faith where heart and hands, mind and body matter equally and the truth of Scripture is confirmed in the truth of the earth. *What Falls from the Sky* is not to be missed.

—*Christina Crook,* author of *The Joy of Missing Out:*
Finding Balance in a Wired World

What Falls from the Sky

What Falls from the Sky

How I Disconnected from the Internet
and Reconnected with the God
Who Made the Clouds

ESTHER EMERY

ZONDERVAN®

ZONDERVAN

What Falls from the Sky
Copyright © 2016 by Esther Emery

Requests for information should be addressed to:
Zondervan, 3900 Sparks Drive SE, Grand Rapids, Michigan 49546

ISBN 978-0-310-34514-5 (ebook)

Library of Congress Cataloging-in-Publication Data

Names: Emery, Esther, author.
Title: What falls from the sky: how I disconnected from the internet and reconnected
    with the God who made the clouds / Esther Emery.
Description: Grand Rapids, Michigan: Zondervan, [2016]
Identifiers: LCCN 2016022214 | ISBN 9780310345107 (hardcover)
Subjects: LCSH: Emery, Esther. | Christian biography—United States. | Nature—
    Religious aspects—Christianity. | Simplicity—Religious aspects—Christianity.
Classification: LCC BR1725.E5155 A3 2016 | DDC 270.092 [B]—dc23 LC record
    available at https://lccn.loc.gov/2016022214

All Scripture quotations, unless otherwise indicated, are taken from The Holy
Bible, New International Version®, NIV®. Copyright © 1973, 1978, 1984, 2011 by
Biblica, Inc.® Used by permission of Zondervan. All rights reserved worldwide.
www.Zondervan.com. The "NIV" and "New International Version" are trademarks
registered in the United States Patent and Trademark Office by Biblica, Inc.®

Any Internet addresses (websites, blogs, etc.) and telephone numbers in this book are
offered as a resource. They are not intended in any way to be or imply an endorsement
by Zondervan, nor does Zondervan vouch for the content of these sites and numbers
for the life of this book.

All rights reserved. No part of this publication may be reproduced, stored in a
retrieval system, or transmitted in any form or by any means—electronic, mechanical,
photocopy, recording, or any other—except for brief quotations in printed reviews,
without the prior permission of the publisher.

Published in association with D.C. Jacobson & Associates, LLC, an Author
Management Company. www.dcjacobson.com.

Cover design: Brian Bobel
Cover photo: Jovana Rikalo / Stocksy
Interior design: Kait Lamphere

First Printing October 2016 / Printed in the United States of America

For Nick, and the wonder
of second chances

Contents

Prologue

It is winter in California on the night I am pulled over for reckless driving. I am on my way to meet someone, at a hipster bar with red lights and parasols in mai tai cocktails. I am on my way to meet a friend who maybe is a hipster herself, who maybe also used to be my best friend. I once knew why I was going to meet this friend. It had something to do with reconciliation, or forgiveness. I am no longer sure.

I am late to meet her. I am driving the extra distance from the house where I am staying since I left my own three weeks ago, thirty miles up the road in this desert land where the cities line up on the freeway like knots on a string . . . thirty miles from the dark house where my husband of six years is sleeping with my toddler son in the heirloom crib his daddy made.

I am burning down the distance on the freeway in a borrowed car, burning through the space between the cities. My friend Missy's car has more power than mine does. I push it a little harder, and then a little harder. I like the way the vibration goes up my arms. I press the needle up, past 100, past 110. I am darting around other cars like a video game.

I will contest the ticket later, in court. I will note my previously perfect driving record, my perfect citizenship. I have never had a speeding ticket in my life. The judge will look at the paper in his hand. He will say, "Ma'am, you were clocked at 113 miles per hour. That is not an oversight." I will sputter. I will want to explain. There will be nothing that I can explain.

When the red and white lights come up around me, I don't know what they are. I don't know where I am. The cop uses short sentences through the electronic bullhorn. "Exit here." "Turn right." "Pull into this gas station." "Turn off the engine." He shines his flashlight in my window and growls, "How much have you had to drink?"

I laugh. It is the kind of laugh that dares him to make things any worse than they already are. I have not had anything to drink. Nor will I. I am stone cold sober, and he doesn't have any idea why I think this is so funny.

He stares at me. Considers. Takes my license. And then he is gone. He is gone for a long time. I don't know when he will be back. I start to look around. I am parked under a tree, and I am not allowed to go anywhere, and there is nothing at all to look at. I begin to realize that there are tiny brown leaves, yellow leaves, yellow-brown leaves falling on the windshield of my borrowed car. They are in slow motion, slipping against the windshield wipers.

I do not suddenly remember that I have precious things to hope for. I do not suddenly regret everything that has happened or feel in any way encouraged for the future. But I have come to a stop. I have come to rest, and there is feeling coming back into my body, starting with my hands, which I realize are shaking. I realize that I might be starting to cry. I reach for my phone, and I am about to text this person who is no longer my best friend in the hipster bar with the red lights and the mai tai cocktails, but instead I tap a different number. And I am texting now, one letter at a time like we had to in those days: "C-a-n-I-c-o-m-e-h-o-m-e-?"

My husband's response is immediate. "Y-e-s-." I wonder if he was holding his phone in his hand. I wonder if he was thinking about me right at that moment, hoping that I would come back, hoping that we would have a chance to try again. I imagine his relief, and it is my own relief.

The officer has written out my court summons and is passing it through the window. I sign, in the presence of the officer. I turn the key in the ignition. I drive the borrowed car back to my own house, where my husband is waiting for me, and my toddler son is still sleeping in his crib. The cop follows me the entire way.

This is the beginning.

PART ONE

the Snow

One

Chasing Tigers

Though I had only one speeding ticket in my life, my ten years spent in Southern California were generally reckless ones. I spent those years chasing tigers in ferocious pursuit of my dreams as a creative career woman, a director and stage manager of plays. The stage was my adopted home, my second family, and the place where I had met my husband a decade before, as we both excelled in college theater at the University of Idaho. From there and from then on, ambition kept us moving rapidly from one short-term gig to another with breathless urgency. Newspaper critics found us talented, inspiring. I was once called a "wunderkind." But still I kept chasing those tigers. There was always a bigger and a better dream.

Mine was not a rock star life, by anyone's measure. But it was a young, ambitious life. I liked moving fast. I liked the way it felt to move fast. I moved so fast, sometimes, that moments or days or weeks all ran together in a kind of blur. One day I opened my eyes and saw that blur and I thought, "Am I missing it? Is this my whole life passing by, and I'm missing it?" And then somewhere right in there I had a spectacular crash.

That's what this story is about. This story is about the point when you're rushing through your life and something brings you to a stop. Maybe coming to a stop is unexpected and very painful. Maybe when you come to a stop, you see some things you don't want to see and think about some things you don't want to think about. But this also happens: after a while you can hear yourself breathing, and you realize that feeling is coming back into your hands.

This is a story about having lived your whole life on a kind of superhighway, with lights and cities and people all rushing past you in a blur . . . and then what it feels like to get off that highway.

I don't know that I could have done it without crashing. The funny thing about getting off that highway is that you absolutely cannot accomplish it by giving the car more gas, which was the only thing I had really been trained to do. I never knew what it would be like to rest, until I came to a rest, so it wasn't as though I could lay out my strategy of how to get there in twelve easy steps. What I did, basically, is I jumped. I got everything broken in my life that could possibly get broken, and then I decided to go for a year without the Internet.

This is a story about a person going for a year without the Internet. It is the story of an elder child of the Net Generation—a blogger, social-networking addict, and fully immersed citizen of the World Wide Web—going for one whole year without electronic communication of any kind. This is a story about navigating the modern world without access to the conveniences of the modern world and how that can change the way you see just about everything.

The thing I most couldn't believe about life without all my screens is just how big the sky is, and how vibrant and demanding are the seasons in New England—at least if you're the fool sitting by the window with neither an iPhone nor a laptop in your lap. I started thinking about these old rhythms of cold and heat, dark and light, and it reminded me of an old Dr. Seuss storybook from my childhood in which a grumpy old king grows tired of the snow, the rain, the sun, and the fog. He asks for his magicians to make up something else, but then the invention goes all wrong—terribly, hilariously wrong—and he wishes for nothing more than his old weather back, exactly the way it was.

This is a story told in four parts, one each for the snow, the rain, the sun, and the fog, four ordinary but astonishingly precious things we receive from the sky.

If you've heard it said that God can be found in the silence, or that silence can be found in God, then it is fair to say that I found both at the same time. I didn't always distinguish between the two, and sometimes I still don't. But the thing I came to realize was just how possible it is—even in this modern world—to give yourself up to both. And what extraordinary, miraculous healing might come for you if you do. The spiritual life, as it found me, was not a journey toward something far away and hard to reach so much as it was the willingness to let go of one hundred and ten distractions, and the courage to let fall one thousand walls between me and the sky. It was the radical simplicity of looking up.

This is a story about going all still and quiet—and how that changes you.

The winter night that I almost crashed on a California freeway was a year before all this begins. There is little record of that intervening year, which was numb and broken and wild with change. But these things happened, in this order: I moved back in with my husband, I quit my career that I loved, we had another baby, and we moved away from California to the very opposite corner of the country. I quit the career because I felt I needed to, to recover the marriage. I had the baby because I was already pregnant, all that time, even the night that I almost crashed in Missy's car. And we moved away from California to the very opposite corner of the country because even broken people can hope for a fresh start.

Why I moved back in with my husband is less clear. As a couple we had been sheared right through. My husband, after six years of marriage, had betrayed me with my best friend. And before that I had strayed too, not once but twice, in almost but not entirely emotional affairs, both times with actors I was directing. There is always a juggling act with career and marriage and kids. In our case we just spectacularly dropped it all. And yet, for reasons that were hardly clear to anyone, least of all us, we did not give up. We kept hanging out near each other, though the air was full of sharp things. And we kept our little family together, despite the cost.

Nick got a job at the stage production company associated with Harvard University. Together, we drove from California to New England, where we rented the bottom half of a shabby red two-family outside of Boston, with a postage-stamp front yard and a chain-link fence.

My idea to go for a year without the Internet came on a whim. It came about much more lightly than was by any measure appropriate, given all this talk of crisis and misery and loss. And it gave no clue that it would lead to any action of true substance, let alone my reconversion to the Christian faith I had long ago left behind. But God is like that, planting little seeds in jokes. And hope is like that too. So often hope shows up looking absolutely ridiculous, if only against the sheer size of the opposition.

I had decided, shortly after we arrived in Boston for our life makeover, that I was going to stop having a cell phone. My cell phone had been entirely used for my career, and now I no longer had a career. I didn't like how quiet my phone was, and I didn't like paying money every month for something to make me wonder why it was so quiet. I never take very long between making decisions and acting on them, so pretty much as soon as I thought all this, I was on the phone with a customer service agent named Sam, and then my husband came into the room.

My husband is the strong and silent type. You might think him a cross between a lumberjack and a marble statue if you don't know any better. But I know better. He is also a wit. We have always had funny in common, even when we had nothing else to share, and as I heard Sam's voice in my ear, gearing up to try to convince me that I didn't want to cancel my cell phone service after all, I felt a sudden and unbearably strong urge to make him laugh.

"Here's the deal, Sam," I said. "Don't tell anyone, but I have to cancel because I'm going for an entire year without a cell phone. I've decided to write a book about my amazing adventures."

Nick did smile, slightly, I think. But it was Sam who got my full attention then. She dropped her sales script and said, "Are you serious? I would totally read that book."

It would not be true to say that Sam's interest didn't capture my imagination. Nor would it be true to say I wasn't at least a bit fascinated by the idea of pulling a stunt that might get me a lot of attention from the world. But also I had a true desire to leave the Internet.

I was tired, tired, tired of the pace I had been keeping—as a career woman and a mom and a person—and for half of it I blamed my screens. I felt my social networking might be crossing some kind of boundary into addiction. I felt all my interactions might be tainted by some shade of the inauthentic. I wondered if I was doomed to spend the best years of my life having stupid arguments in comment threads.

I kept swiping and tapping and scrolling with what seemed an increasingly frantic pace. And beneath it all, I felt a kind of creeping numbness, a profound feeling of disconnection. At times I felt strangely unreal, as if I might be able to swipe my hand right through my own body.

In my imagination, the fictional experiment began to grow and take a shape. What if I were to go an entire year not only without a cell phone but without electronic communication of any kind? No data, no e-mail, no texting, no Internet use at all? I was quite sure that I could do it. Stubborn and steadfast are qualities I have. Cultural criticism is my favorite thing to do. And a year of isolation seemed a strangely perfect fit for what would already be, for me, a year of doubling down.

Before hitting crisis, I had never intentionally been unemployed. An overachiever since the cradle, I had graduated high school at age fifteen, started working full-time at age sixteen, and never let my pace drop even briefly since. But this year, for all the hardest and most important reasons, I planned to stay at home with my two tiny children, cultivating rest and relationship and much needed family values, all in a new-to-me and unfamiliar town.

We had moved to Boston so Nick could work in the scenery department at American Repertory Theater, where he would draft and cost the sets, lead crews, and occasionally build something spectacular with his own hands. It was the work of his hands that made Nick fall in love with technical theater years ago. He made beautiful things in the context of imaginary worlds. But since then he has risen through the ranks. Now he works in the office, insanely long hours under tremendous pressure, carrying administrative responsibility at one of the most accomplished and acclaimed regional theaters in the country.

As his wife, at this stage in his development, it is my part to eat dinner alone with my little ones as Nick stays out in late-night technical rehearsals and notes sessions. In some ways this arrange-ment suits me perfectly. There are still sharp things in the air between me and my husband and land mines between our feet. Sometimes I actually would rather blog, or read blogs, or crochet tiny slightly misshapen mittens for my children than hang out with the man who so recently broke my heart. Other times I find the total separation between his life and mine completely unbearable.

I don't always know which one of me is which.

I know this much: I need a project. I desperately need a really, really, really big project, something I can sink my teeth into, something that will keep me occupied, something that can restore context and meaning to a life that has come undone at all the seams.

Of course, nobody ever loses everything without gaining some small thing in return. My lose-everything move across the country gave me back two brothers I misplaced years ago, two men who have lived on the Eastern seaboard for a decade or more despite it being so far from where our family originated in Western wilderness. I adore my brothers, and I have lived too far away from them for far too long. They are instantly my entire social network.

The younger of the two, Jacob, lives very near to me and comes over for dinner on Thursday nights, but the older brother, Dan, lives several hours away in New York City, where he is a musician and a successful entrepreneur. When I told Dan my idea to go for a year without the Internet, the first thing he said was, "Wow! That is radical. That is truly radical." But the second thing he said was, "How will you get your writing out?"

First I said, "Well, I won't, Dan. That's kind of the point." But then I completely changed my mind. I dreamed up an epic piece of writing called *The Unblog*, which would be written in installments—not so much like my blogs have always been written in installments, as in the "log" part of Weblog, but more like James Joyce sending out chapters of *Ulysses*. It would be an incentive for people to write me letters. See, if you send me a letter, then I'll send you an episode of the *Unblog*, which will be a real physical item that you have that nobody else has. Who can pass up a chance like that? My mailbox will overflow.

The first installment will go to my friend Missy, back in California, who I think will be deeply, deeply into this. If I were going to have a fan club, I would want Missy to be the president. Who else would participate in that fan club is unclear. But they must exist. If you have a blog, you must have a readership. If you have an *Unblog*, you must have a radical, eclectic fan base made up of people who wear a lot of black and cook with nutritional yeast and practice nonviolent resistance.

When I look out the window and the silence comes in, it's going to make me feel very silly about all this. The vast peace of the sky is going to suggest to me, gently, that perhaps I should stop blogging, now that I am not on the Internet and therefore no longer have a blog. Also, it will make me want to crawl under my desk and desperately want to become a better person.

But as I begin my Year Without Internet, I am not thinking of any of this. I am not looking through my windows at the sky. I am not thinking about the hugeness of things that are not me. I'm just trying to find a way to live a life that matters. I'm trying to find a way to feel my life.

The first thing I feel is a kind of emptiness. It is only five o'clock on the last day of November 2009, but dusk is already overtaking my living room as I make the phone call to turn off the Internet service in my house.

The customer service agent is in a perky mood. He tells me that if I bundle my cable phone service with cable television, I can reduce my monthly bill. I think this is hilarious because I don't have a television—if I were to want to watch something, I would generally think to use my laptop—but he says that doesn't matter, it's just cheaper this way. Then he explains, in his perky voice, "When I reset the service, this line will go dead."

And then that happens. There is silence on the line. This will be my only indication that the Year Without Internet has begun.

Later I will wish I had given myself more of a send-off. Maybe some balloons or bubbles or a big ribbon, like the opening of a store. But there was plenty of action on the Internet, where I blogged a countdown to fanfare and applause. I pronounced my intentions on all my social media. On my Facebook page I put up a status with my mailing address and then another one with this cheerful message: "I'm not here, but you are. Hi."

I thought that was clever.

The first morning of the first day of the Year Without Internet is not very much like a life-changing miracle. I spend it all in the children's section of the library, where two-year-old Milo looks at books and Baby Stella chews on a pink hippopotamus. It seems peaceful enough. But as the morning goes on, I become more and more obsessed with a certain image of myself. It is the image of me as I appear on the Internet, and I am painfully aware that it is slipping out of my control.

Should I have put that stupid note up on Facebook? Over the course of an entire year, will I come to regret that? I've put something even stupider on my Google profile, which will supposedly show up if anybody Googles me. Will anybody Google me? What if somebody Googles me and all they see is this completely awkward phrase, which quite obscures the complexity of my intentions? They won't be getting a message from the real me. They'll be getting a message from the false me, the impostor—my cyber self gone rogue.

I charge at one of the library computers like a television SWAT team. I am on the Google profile page in seconds, where I erase the offending comment, and only a slow load saves me from my Facebook page, which I have just begun to access when I come to my senses and log off.

I back away from the computer like it's a dangerous animal. I have been working on this project for a month. I have planned and prepared and announced and exuded self-confidence. And all it took to change my mind was a ten-second encounter with my vanity and a Google profile?

It is well after noon when I open a word-processing document to spin this shocking early failure into a dramatic opening install-ment of the *Unblog*. I find that I have double clicked on the Web browser icon—by accident and by habit—and watch helplessly as the computer attempts to access the Internet. Thankfully it finds no connection and tells me so.

I breathe in gratitude and consider taking banana bread to all my neighbors, with the urgent plea that they refrain at all costs from getting unsecured wireless.

Like an overloaded computer, I go into safe mode. I read a little. I drink a little tea. I hang out with my kids. I wonder if anyone has Googled me today and, if so, if they thought I seemed intelligent.

On Day Two I read a bit of a book and try using the phone book. On Day Three I use a paper map and read almost half of an entire book. That night I see too clearly in my mind's eye a scene from a Shakespearean tragedy I had watched at my husband's place of employment. The image of a screaming Lady Macbeth seems so real I almost bump into her, and I realize that my brain has captured whole sections of the play with impressive precision.

I feel crazy—and simultaneously awesome. Maybe this is how those genius artists of the history books always felt. Where I had the Internet, with its obsessive photographers and iconographers and the steady stream of attacking, flashing advertisements, now I have something I am learning to call silence.

Concentration is hard to come by. I dip into a book by the window, but then I feel that I don't like that book. I never liked that book. I sit down at the computer, only to hop back up because I am not actually interested in playing computer solitaire. I lie down in my room, just for a minute, until Milo takes that as a signal that it is time to play a game of Airplane. I arch up like a serpent and hiss, "Do. Not. Touch. Me."

"Mama's a dragon," Milo says cheerfully as I put down a plate of toast next to the soup to complete our unromantic dinner for two. Nick is working late into the evening, which is normal, and Stella is in the play gym a few feet away, peacefully spinning the circus tent.

"What does a dragon do?" I ask.

"*Rawwrrr*," he says, showing his teeth. "Dragon does *rawwrrr*."

This is alarming, but also inconclusive. He likes dragons.

But the conclusion is unmistakable on Day 10, when my husband is finally home for dinner and the meal is silent. After dinner he says, "I'm going to take a shower. There's nothing else to do."

I snap back, "There's a load of laundry in the dryer."

"Noted," he says. And I hear the sound of his footsteps going down the hall.

I feel as if I just got a glimpse of myself in the mirror and found that I am someone I don't like.

When I open the door the next evening to my brother Jacob, it is like letting in a different world. He is the Pied Piper, the playful bachelor uncle draped in long scarves that Milo loves to grab and pull and chase. He hasn't even begun to take off his coat before the two of them are playing some kind of a game, one that involves running and giggling but is otherwise totally incomprehensible to outsiders.

Baby Stella joins in the giggling from her high chair, coyly dropping her potato masher for her charming uncle to pick up. What if I drop this? Will you give it back? Oh, you did! What if I drop this? Will you give it back? Oh, you did!

I feel the ease of color bursting onto the gray December sky. I am relieved, relaxed. Jacob is my nearest-in-age brother. We were as close as any two people could be when we were growing up, but we landed in different places in our late teens and haven't lived near each other since. It is by sheer luck and miracles that he lives here, in this town that I moved to for my husband's job. Like Nick, he is employed by Harvard University. And he is the closest thing I have to a friend.

Tonight we're having the closest thing I can have to a party. Our niece Beth is also studying in Boston for this semester, and Nick and I have invited her and Jacob to help with the decorating of our Christmas tree. The tree is very pretty. We have every kind of hot beverage you can think of. We eat leftover cake from Beth's December birthday, and we string popcorn and cranberries into garlands. I am very efficient at this. My popcorn never breaks. I am a master popcorn stringer. I cannot be unseated in my master popcorn-stringer-ness. Until we run out of popcorn, and I duck into the back bedroom, away from my family who are also my guests, and cry.

I'm sorry, I say to my imaginary audience, I can't do it. I can't perform anything at all. I can't explain anything. I can't speak, I can't write, I can't cook, and I can't tell you why I'm going for a Year Without Internet.

On Super Saturday, the biggest shopping day of the year, my husband turns thirty-three years old. He stumbles out of bed at dawn, lurches to the sink, and begins furiously washing dishes. Milo and I, who are usually up at this hour, coax him down and into a kitchen chair. We have a performance to do. We have been practicing our song for weeks. It is the "Happy Birthday" song, but sung in two parts, as a responsorial sort of thing, modeled after *Winnie the Pooh.*

Nick smiles, is visibly touched, and then goes right back to doing dishes. It isn't until later that he tells me about the recurring dream in which he keeps getting older but never grows up, and I realize this is why he hurled himself into domestic hard labor at the sink. He is trying to out-clean his mortality.

But I have little room for sympathy. I am run ragged by a two-page-long holiday food-shopping list, a birthday dinner, and a three-layer, from-scratch birthday cake I make because Nick's mother always made it, not to mention an obsession with how we should arrange our furniture.

Nick has given me an early Christmas gift. It took a spectacular amount of effort on his part, with no cell phone and no Internet, and, even if it didn't, it is still a spectacular gift: a half-century-old record player with cabinet. Beth, my college-aged niece, immediately dubbed it "The Coolest Thing Ever."

It is also five and a half feet wide. I can't figure out how to make it fit with all our other furniture. I can't figure out how to make anything fit. Christmas is six days away, and both my brothers are coming to stay in our little house, and I am coming clean into panic.

Since I don't have the Internet, I am doing all my Christmas shopping in person, using a phone book to locate the store and a paper map to get there. This is a huge project, which for my workaholic personality should be as much a relief as a source of stress.

But at my very first store, I realize that my debit card qualifies as electronic communication. I don't know what to do. I never even thought about it before. *Please*, I tell the perfectionist in me, *please just let me get through Christmas.*

Why does nothing go the way it is supposed to go? My husband has to think about his mortality while I am busy gifting him with cute little birthday songs. My record player is great, but I would have liked it better if I'd known it was coming. And my no-Internet experiment is totally off the tracks.

I came all the way out here, to this Internet-free island, because I wanted to feel something. I wanted a richer experience of life. But I don't feel anything. All I feel is numbness and motion. I spin out from myself and look down and see this figure trying to scratch and claw and grab at the world. I am running and waving my arms madly as I draw close to something that frightens me, which is still inarticulate but has something to do with being alone with myself.

Whatever it is, it makes me really scared.

After I have returned from buying everything on my two-page shopping list and we are all together in the kitchen, preparing the birthday meal, Nick tries to stop me. He puts his arms around me, trying to be with me, trying to bring my heart rate down to match his, and both our feet to match the speed of the turning of the earth. Stella is cackling and banging a cake pan against the tray of her high chair. Milo is standing on a stool sifting the dry ingredients. He is a ticking cake flour time bomb. I break the embrace. I'm thinking about everything I ought to do to make the birthday experience go the way it is supposed to go, and then the Christmas experience, because all this is so important, and before it's too late.

"Time isn't waiting for us," I say to Nick. "We've got to move."

But, of course, I am completely wrong about that.

I dream in the night of a near apocalyptic landscape of white. When I wake up, I open the curtains to white, fluffy, sound-absorbing snowfall, and I wonder how in my sleep I could have known.

Nick likes the snow. It brightens him up. It makes the lines and edges of him more distinct. He goes out while the snow is still falling and starts shoveling the driveway, and then the walk and steps, and then the neighbor's walk and steps.

Milo is shockingly quiet, for a two-year-old. We are a matched pair, he and I, at different windows, both staring, I at the snow itself and he at Daddy on the driveway with the snow shovel. The baby is asleep in her crib, and Nick's snow shoveling seems to take hours. I had known the snow was coming and, skittish Californian that I am, prepared my pantry for a siege. I have no place to go, nothing to do, and no companion except for my son's wordless wonder at this new thing that falls from the sky.

I take down my camera and photograph my son. I take dozens of pictures; rather, I take the same picture dozens of times. He ignores me. I make some hot cocoa and reach my hand into the empty cookie jar and wonder when Nick is going to come back inside and bake something. Finally I fall into a chair by the window and pick up a slim volume of philosophy in which the author churns academic scholarship with Christian theology to arrive at the following chilling accusation: "Only someone who has lost the spiritual power to be at leisure can be bored."*

I let the book fall into my lap, and the whiteness and soundlessness of the snow wrap around the walls and slide down into my throat. I try to imagine "the spiritual power to be at leisure," and I don't know what that is, but I know that whatever it is, it is something I want. I want it in a way that is crushing and inarticulate, like the way I wanted to hold my newborn babies, or the way I

---

*Josef Pieper, *Leisure: The Basis of Culture*, trans. Gerald Malsbary (South Bend, IN: St. Augustine's Press, 1998), 54.

wanted to reach out into the broken air to save my marriage. It is as if something has just come undone, deep in the bottom of me, some constricting tie loosed . . . or just one brick removed from a thick wall between me and the sky.

Milo plays in the living room, and the baby sleeps, and time passes around us, and when Nick finally comes back inside, smiling from his own snowy adventure, I feel strange and loose and liquid. I feel absurdly, hugely grateful for the snow.

By the time Stella wakes up, one of three things has happened: the furniture has shrunk, or my tolerance has grown, or two days is just enough time to get used to things. Nick goes out on snowy roads to buy me a secondhand painting that he says he is sure I will love. I am openly skeptical. I am much too picky for that sort of thing, for art to be coming into my house without having been properly vetted and scrutinized. But then the picture arrives, and I do love it. We now have an original painting on the wall over the five-foot-wide record player, which my husband picked up at the neighborhood Goodwill. And I like it. I like the whole room. I don't have any idea what just happened to me.

The next day I sit at the computer and stare at the blank page. The *Unblog* isn't working anymore. But I'm not sure it matters.

My hope was that going off my artificial entertainment addiction would tell me what I have never gotten right about Christmas, and about meaning, and about what it takes to keep a family together. I had hoped my experiment would unlock a magic pattern obscured all this time with my running around and being desperate and chasing shiny things.

But so far, all it does is make me feel the things I've lost.

In the afternoon both kids sleep and my brother Jacob comes over and tells me about a study in the field of human psychology.

This is normal. Jacob is many things, among them, extremely well informed. He passes as a New England intellectual, though in truth he was born in rural Idaho, like me, into the same unusual family. We are both strangers in this strange land, but he has come ahead to learn the customs, and he faithfully visits me on Thursday nights and on occasional weekday afternoons to ensure that my brain doesn't atrophy from lack of use.

Study participants, Jacob explains, were asked to make an exhaustive list of the people from whom they could ask a small favor. The total number turned out to be, with some consistency, 150. Jacob explains that this appears to be the maximum number of friends that a person can have at one time. We are somehow wired to have no more than 150 friends.

He goes on to speculate about optimum community size: the size of a group in which everybody can be friends with everybody else. But I am trying to count my 150 friends. Missy, Jo, Janet, Delicia . . . I had 407 Facebook friends when I went off the Internet. I wonder if I still have 407 Facebook friends. I wonder if I should send Missy my password so she can log on to my Facebook account and accept friend requests, just in case my project is taking off and I'm finally starting to get famous.

I once asked a friend, after he was laid off from his job, what he was doing with his time. He said, "I've almost finished reading the Internet."

I can't stop thinking about the snow and the feeling of rest, which was so unfamiliar and so much like coming home. The Internet begins to come into focus not as a unique entity but as one of a giant family of providers of busy work: busy work being defined as any work that we do that we don't really want to get done. I could surf the Internet. I could pick lint off my sweater.

That is a certain kind of rest. It is not rest like that snowy Sunday when silence fell into my lap, and the whole world came to a pause in its spinning, and I decided the record player was okay right where it was. It is not my brain sitting down by the window, but it is my brain getting sent away from me, with a lollipop, so at least it will stop tugging at my clothes. Here's a labyrinth for you, brain, and here's a riddle. Have a nice time. Let me know when you're done, and I'll give you something else to do. Don't worry, I'll never run out of tasks. I'll keep you busy.

I sit down to nurse Stella. When she is done, I have no place in particular to be. I look at her. She looks at me. We are a perfect fit for each other, and the whole world waits on us. Why do I not more often stop right here?

It seems like all one long suspended moment, all the way to the day before the day before Christmas, when Nick gets home early from work and we begin our Christmas holiday. I'm more relaxed than I have been in I don't know how long, and the tension between us fades into the sheer familiarity of domestic work. I am a nervous cook, but an extremely opinionated one. I taste everything. Nick does all the actual work. He hardly leaves the kitchen all evening, making cinnamon rolls and French bread, as I plan kid-friendly activities and select Christmas records to be played on our "Coolest Thing Ever" record player. In the morning our guests arrive, and we string more popcorn and cranberries, and this time we don't run out of popcorn.

For Christmas Eve I convince Nick to go with me to a holiday service at a big, grand church in the Back Bay. I have for many years been an infrequent churchgoer, but I occasionally go on Christmas Eve. My siblings are uninterested, the children think it is boring, and I don't honestly think Nick has ever been. But I am in active search of a Christmas with true meaning, and something nags at me that I won't be satisfied unless I can sing, in candlelight, "Joy to the World."

The church is beautiful. It's old. It's the sort of architecture that makes people from the West Coast look around for a white-coated attendant or a ticket line, but I know from a phone call to a friend that this is a real church that people use. My friend is Presbyterian, and so is the church she recommended, but the denomination means little to me and that much less to Nick. My religious heritage is mixed to the point of being unrecognizable. More to the point, the Jesus part of my faith is lost completely to cynicism these last twelve years. My husband is quite simply an atheist. But he is pleased tonight to be right where he is, with his wife on his arm in a pretty dress. He is pleased that I finally asked him for something and gave him half a chance to answer yes.

The Christmas Eve service is lush with carols. I sing a lot, loudly. Nick will tell me later, "You sounded good." But I also drift away between rousing choruses into a Christmas melancholy. I look at the people who fill the pews—people I've never seen before, all people I couldn't call by name. I wish for my 150 people who are scattered across the miles and the years. I wish for my 150 people who can't be here tonight because they are too far away, or because I failed to invite them, or, in the case of the ones waiting for me back at my own house, because no carol or candle calls them through the doors of a Christian church.

I stand with all the others, and I sing, and I dream of a room filled with all my people, a room big enough for the different faith traditions and the radical aggressive agnosticism and the love. It is a fantasy, my magic gathering room, and it also is the Internet. My 150 people are there tonight. I wonder if they miss me.

Back at home we do our own Christmas storytelling by the tree. I ask each of the kids what they want to do. Eight-year-old Elijah, my nephew, will sing "The Twelve Days of Christmas." His little sisters, Neoma and Aviv, will do a little dance, accompanied by Uncle Jacob on the ukulele. Milo wants to sing his song too, and at first I think he's making things up because he's only two years old, but then I realize that he knows exactly what song he's talking about, and so do I.

We go first, because he's the youngest, and I kneel with my arms around him beside the lit-up tree as we sing the "Happy Birthday" song just the way we practiced it, to Jesus.

After the kids are in bed, we stay up late into the night with my brothers, completely destroying ourselves with laughter over the illustrations in a vintage children's book. Dan and his wife, Miriam, sleep in our bed, and Nick and I sleep in the living room, under the tree, and Jacob curls his six-foot frame onto a couch cushion that fits just perfectly between the dining room table and the record player.

In the morning Milo is the first one up. Nick lifts him up to touch the foil-wrapped cardboard star at the top of the tree, as I am positioned with the cord at the outlet to "magically" turn on the Christmas lights. Jacob looks up and gives it all a groggy smile from the dining room floor. The presents almost ruin everything, but not quite, and Jacob eats the Coca-Cola ham (even though he is a vegetarian) that Miriam prepared (even though she is Jewish). It is a beautiful, unbroken white Christmas.

The next day we wave good-bye to our guests, who are off to have adventures in places with Wi-Fi as I hold on to one of Nick's arms with both of mine. Later we will watch *Jewel of the Nile* on a DVD checked out from the library and drink leftover wine and make out on the floor in front of the Christmas tree. Later my husband will tell me that we are like a re-glued plate, maybe even stronger than before. But just now I am watching my brother's red Subaru back out of the driveway into the expanse of my first New England winter and wondering how it has happened that Christmas is over already.

I get back to the computer a few days later, but I know there will be no more installments to the *Unblog*. Something is different. The story is changed. The craving for the Internet has dissipated. I don't spend my days thinking of how things would be different if only I were online. What I do think about is Me. Me is everywhere. Me is all around me, like the expanse of fluffy sound-absorbing snow. I can't get away from Me. And Me is not someone with whom I am terribly impressed.

I don't know why I don't rest. I don't know why I can't be more satisfied with what I have and less grasping toward everything else for whatever it is that is supposed to make me happy. But I also know that I am not the only one. When Milo gets a plush Eeyore as a trailing hand-me-down gift the day after Christmas, he doesn't say thank you. Instead, he looks greedily around the room and says, "Where's Pooh?"

We are all looking for more.

I go swimming all day long in a sea of inconsequential details. I search for the thing that matters. All day long I am chasing tigers, which is looking for God, which is looking for the face of my significance. I don't want to do this anymore. This is my New Year's resolution. But it's too hard to explain. "Be a better person" is too vague, and "Stop accepting easy answers when only complicated ones will do" doesn't fit on a piece of scratch paper. So I write down "No debit card."

And I hope that will be enough.

Two

My Year
Under a Rock

I t is a feature of a university job, like the one my husband now
holds, that scattered between the long stretches of working
ridiculously long hours and hardly being able to breathe for the
stress, there are strange opposing sequences known as vacations.
The Harvard University winter vacation is three weeks long—
three weeks for me and Nick to be in a house together, with no
Internet.

Nick goes out grocery shopping every single day. This is in part
to keep from going stir crazy in our boring wireless-free house, but
it is also because he likes to cook and bake. He recently has been
rapidly expanding his baking skills, perhaps to keep from going stir
crazy in our boring wireless-free house. He brings me cinnamon
rolls and bread as well as *Sesame Street* records that he and Milo
bought at the Goodwill for twenty-five cents apiece. He brings them
like offerings.

I devote myself like an acolyte to the silence.

If I am going to be spending this much time with myself, some things about me are going to have to change. I'm going to have to be nicer. I'm going to have to be more disciplined. And I'm going to have to be more interesting.

I rise before dawn like a monk, and in the darkness around my desk, self-improvement resolutions multiply like dust bunnies. I will wake before dawn. I will practice silence. I will not run away from things that scare me. I will practice juggling and photography. I will learn how to play an instrument and speak a language. I will read all the big books I have always meant to read. And I will stop eating so many cinnamon rolls.

I begin a notebook in which I will document my progress. I will write down what chapters I've read, what letters I've written, and how many minutes I've spent in silent contemplation. The notebook itself is a comic choice. The logo on the front says "Wired™," and on the inside cover is a list of Web-related keyboard shortcuts. The marketing team must have said, "Let's make paper products that are digital friendly and computer hip." It's like crying out in the streets the succession of the monarchy. "Long live the king! The king is dead!"

I read a couple chapters in a book, write a letter by hand, spend quality time with my two-year-old, and note all this like a score card in the pocket-sized cornflower blue notebook. Later, lying like a good novitiate in my bed at 10:00 p.m., I think how funny people are, that we go in search of deep meaning and then think we can measure it in chapters.

It is time, I am now convinced, for me to write something for the Internet. The *Unblog* may be dead (long live the *Unblog*), but I have at this point gone an entire month without using the Internet, and it seems downright irresponsible to fail to report this accomplishment to somebody.

I write a little thing, which is not *exactly* a blog post, although it has some attributes in common with a blog post, namely that it is a short personal essay created for the purpose of being posted on the World Wide Web. I save it onto a memory stick, put the memory stick in a manila envelope, and mail it with four stamps to a friend in California, along with instructions for how she can post it to my blog.

I don't know what will come of this, if anything. It will be at least three days before Amy receives it, and days more before she puts it up, because she is a free spirit and not one to get all stressed out by doing things in a hurry. Then it will be three days more after that before I see any responses in my mailbox.

Or, just as likely, forever.

Outside, the wind shifts to bitter. The snow becomes hard and glaring. I stay inside for days. The wind sucks all the color out of the street, as the house fills up with warm smells and yeasty concoctions and an endless supply of golden cinnamon rolls. Nick takes Milo outside to make snowmen, again, and then back to the Goodwill, again, and to the grocery store, again, again. I drink cup after cup of hot cocoa and stay close to the furniture.

I have a memory of snow that was soft and white and silent. It was my meditative chamber and a shelter for tender growing things that go dormant in winter. But the snow outside no longer bears the slightest resemblance. What used to be pure and white and silent is now crusty and laced with brown and black, and probably something peed on it. What used to be divine and heaven sent is now utterly a thing of this world, all mixed up with car exhaust and the neighbors' bad manners, and getting into the cracks of the cars themselves and making my fingers hurt.

And then Nick goes back to work.

This is how fast a truth can shift: a beautiful thing can turn on you. One moment I am resting and holding my babies, and it's all very beautiful and profound. The next I'm housebound in the most unhealthy way, starved for stimulus, and thinking I might start taking in stray cats.

In the mail I receive a half-sized manila envelope from Kirsten Brandt, a successful contemporary theater director whose triumphs were once an inspiration to me. She remembers me as a professional colleague and treats me accordingly, a memory apparently clearer in her mind than in mine. She has written to me about the effects of digital communication on society, asking, "How do we have real conversations? How do we prompt dialogues?"

Possibly as an attempt to do just that, she sent me some images of an artist she thinks I might like. I have only glanced at the print-outs when my eyes lock on the URL printed in the corner of each page, and I observe with neither scientific method nor detachment that I am salivating.

And this is how it happens. Solitude makes her subtle shift into loneliness. A loner becomes a shut-in. Somewhere in here I probably really should have called someone, but what would I say? "Hey, Jacob, could you come over? I'm starting to feel like taking in stray cats."

Two months ago, when I first announced my project, my sister-in-law, Miriam, stood in my pantry and said, "Your San Diego friends won't write you letters. They won't pick up the phone as easily as they might contact you on e-mail or Facebook, and you can't expect them to. My concern is that you might become isolated, and that could lead to becoming depressed."

Stirring polenta over my stove a few days later, Jacob said, "I would think, having just moved to a new place and otherwise lacking a support network, that this could block avenues for communication that you might later find you want."

I answered them both with blog posts. I am introverted, lousy at maintaining friendships, and a little afraid of people. When I allowed myself, I processed every relationship through a screen.

It was 2005 when I found the blogosphere. I was looking for a Web installation artwork called "We Feel Fine" that I had heard about on public radio, which was billed as an "exploration of human emotions in six movements." At the time I was working on writing a play, and human emotion is like the inkwell in which you dip the pen. I remember. I flopped down on the bed in my studio apartment with my cat and my laptop and the bright red bougainvillea outside the window, and I waited for the applet to load. (In those days it was quite normal to wait for things to load.)

The background was hot pink, and when I clicked on the first movement, it brought up a collection of brightly colored dots swimming madly all over the screen. If you could catch one of those dots and click on it, it would bring up a sentence containing the words "I feel," which would be a real sentence, pulled from the blog of a real person, somewhere, that you otherwise would never know or see or meet.

"I feel better now."

"I feel trapped."

"I saw untold beauty silent magnificent beauty that made my heart sing and cry tears of joy at the same time and what did I feel in essence?"

"I feel like I should switch to a different shampoo."

I watched it for hours. I clicked and clicked and clicked and clicked on those goofy little swarming dots. I should have known right then.

I moved on from there to the Hype Machine, which was another blog aggregator that scanned the Web for blog posts with attached music files. That transformed my music collection and along with it my coolness factor. I made mixes of the most current, most unknown, most awesome tracks in indie music, and, strange beyond belief for a person who had always been a bit of a nerd, I was suddenly the one in the room who was "in the know."

That little affair came to an end with a band called Arcade Fire. One day the whole music blogosphere went over their heads for Arcade Fire—all at once, kind of like a timer had gone off—and I couldn't figure out what they were talking about. Either it was their taste that could no longer be trusted or it was my own.

That's the exact moment when I started thinking about the word *authenticity*. I started wondering about good taste, and mass appeal, and how much time bloggers might spend counting page hits. It occurred to me suddenly how these bloggers might move as a pack, shifting their content toward the audience that would give them the clicks they craved. But it was too late for me then. I had already fallen in.

For the next five years the blogosphere grew as I grew more and more attached to it. Usually I was a lurker, a stalker, a reader, but occasionally a writer too. In my countdown to going off the Internet, I wrote a blog called *The Internet Binge*, which was simply descriptive. For one month I spent as much time as I wanted on the Internet. I spread my gray matter willy-nilly around the Web. I checked my e-mail continuously, like a bar-pressing test monkey. I stalked blogs from one coast to the other, and I wrote on my own blog every day. I wrote it like a letter to a friend.

I wrote about the quality of connection between souls and what a loss I feel when social behavior is squished into sound bytes and distributed like products to consumers. I wrote how strange it is that we think happy lives are dependent on this new technology that is barely old enough to buy itself a drink.

I wrote too about the problem of addiction. I wrote how frightened I have felt that I would miss something, how that feeling was down in my body. When I couldn't check the status of my electronic self, my breath might come a little too fast or my hands would get shaky. I confessed how my particular weaknesses render me particularly vulnerable. I am a performer and a perfectionist, already hooked on the drug of validation and prone to envy. I have anxiety in social situations and feel nervous talking on the phone. The computer offers me a safer, gentler way of being friends.

But can the computer replace what it so effectively imitates? In the last few months before I dropped off the Internet, I had come near to living a wholly electronic life. I was in danger of giving up entirely on real people. My whole life could be virtual. I might behave as though I had never left California at all. Or as though nothing in my broken life has ever fallen apart.

So emerged my position statement, the philosophical heart of the Year Without Internet. I do not believe that advanced communications technology is required to have a full and vibrant connection to the world. I do not believe that I have to be digitally connected in order to be happy. I believe I could do just as well, or maybe better, with something real.

This was my position, but if I were to now want to prove that position right, I would have to get out of my house. I would have to greet people in person, get to know my neighbors, have fascinating experiences, and invite people over for dinner. These are the things that would support my hypothesis. But I don't feel like doing any of those things. Without the *Unblog*, I don't feel motivated to do any of those things . . . because no one is watching.

I wonder if this was true in times before our time. Was it impossible to imagine putting effort into something if there were no eyes to look at it? Was this true that a life seemed meaningless if it was lived in a place where it could not be seen?

In the same mail as Kirsten's letter, I receive my laptop power cord from my brother Dan. We had visited his house in the suburbs of New York City before my experiment began, and I accidentally left my power cord. For the last six weeks I have had to borrow my husband's laptop, which is a kind of neutral territory, without any of my files or my pictures or my personal history. But today my oldest brother has done me the favor of returning functionality to my laptop, and with it the question of what useful thing I am doing with my life.

I had such high hopes. I was going to be Dr. Who hurtling backward through time in a phone booth. I was going to be *Little Women* and *Little House on the Prairie*, all at the same time. I was going to embark on a solitary voyage through dire peril and tempest toss'd seas and end up shipwrecked on a mysterious foreign coastline of new possibilities . . . like the closing sequence of a Hollywood movie I used to love.

I was going to be *famous*.

But in the truth-approaching quiet of my real life, there is no ocean and no ship to sail on, unless it's the snow outside my window or a cornflower blue notebook full of mostly empty pages. Unless Kirsten Brandt takes time out of her busy working life to send me letters or I allow myself a monthly episode of narration to the Internet, I have not much to say and no audience to whom I need to say it.

When I plug in my power cord and the black screen of my laptop lights up, it brings up a social networking page. It is old;

there is no Internet connection. The page will disappear if I hit any command, so I don't. Instead I minimize it, carefully. Hours later, after the kids go to bed, I bring it up again and read every single word, including the advertisements, and then sit on my hands and wonder if that was cheating. I look out at the New England winter outside my window and back to the photo of my newborn daughter on the desktop of my computer. And I know that, yes, in truth, it is isolation that I have come looking for no matter how many times I've said the opposite.

In all the tales of heroes, growth begins with a pilgrimage, like the Grail knights, venturing into the darkest places of the woods. In my tiny, inconsequential modern life, this is my pilgrimage: out from under the shelter of my screens, to see the sky.

On Thursday morning I wake knowing I must absolutely go to the grocery store because Jacob is coming over for dinner, and I must, must leave the house before I become a shut-in for real. The wind is so strong it tosses an empty round trash can down the street. I watch from the window to see how far it will travel and realize there are several trash cans bouncing around in our gutters like a pack of Hollywood urchins. Instead of stuffing my kids into their winter coats, I write a handwritten letter to my friend Jaysen with an open plea for help.

Jaysen is an actor from my old life in Southern California who posts words of wisdom and inspiration on his social networks every single day. He's just like that. He never takes a break from being wise and inspirational. I've had the idea to send him a supply of pre-stamped, self-addressed postcards with the request that he write his wise and inspirational messages in pen on paper and drop them in the mail, and in so doing help save me from being stranded on Arctic ice.

I haven't got any postcards. Milo and I use white cardstock and markers to make them. I make a heart and a star. I make one with the word "Love," in memory of those old stamps from the '80s. I make some blank ones in case Jaysen wants to do some scribbling of his own. Finally I do a scene of four angels and a yellow sun. I smile at that one, because it's cute, and when I put it on a postcard with a stamp, I find myself leaving the address line open. I'm not sure that I want it to return to me. I might want Jaysen to keep it. I might want to give it to him, as a gift.

Then suddenly I jump up and dance around in a circle with Milo, who is two years old and pretty much always up for a little dancing around in a circle, because I realize that I've discovered something about the difference between snail mail and e-mail. I have always known that there was something different about writing letters, something especially fulfilling and rewarding. I used to think it was a matter of appreciating permanence over ephemera, but this is something else. This is the difference between showing and giving. This is the difference between holding on and letting go.

When I write a blog, I keep a hold on all my stories, and my poetry, and my pictures. They are under my fingers still, and I can take down the archives whenever I change my mind. But today, when I mail away this paper-and-marker sketch of four haloed figures and a yellow sun, I don't expect to see it again. I let it go. That's what you do when you write a letter. You make something for somebody else. And then you let it go.

Jacob will tell me later that important people have always kept copies of their letters. He will even tell me about a machine invented by a famous American that would allow him to write two copies of a letter at once while only grasping one pen. So then I'll say, okay, okay, maybe it isn't the mailbox that forces this perspective of generosity. Maybe I found generosity here because generosity is something I've been looking for. Maybe I'm tired of acting like the mythical "economic man" who always pursues the greatest gain for the least amount of effort. Maybe I'm tired of holding my fist so tight my nails dig into my palm. I want to act as if I have enough. I have enough time. I have enough creativity. I have enough paper, and marker ink, to share.

When I first announced my project, a blog-reading friend jokingly called it "Esther's Year Under a Rock." I don't want that to be true, but also it is true. It's true that my broken heart is looking for some kind of shelter.

Still, as much as I am an introvert who avoids face-to-face contact, it seems essential, way past essential, that I continue to go places outside of my house. Sundays are the day that Nick can be home to watch the children and I can try to make some entrée into the community where I live. Scanning the listings in the free newspaper, which I have picked up at the subway station, I settle on a poetry-writing club that meets Sunday mornings at the bagel shop in Somerville.

But then, at the last minute and almost against my will, I find myself getting off the train at Park Street and walking across Boston Common to the church I visited on Christmas Eve.

At first I have no intention to actually go in. I think I'm just bagging out on the poetry club because of my social anxiety, taking some kind of a relaxing solitary walk. I have been nothing but an outspoken critic of Christianity for a good twelve years, ever since I walked away from the faith and didn't look back. It is not my own doing, or my own will, that brings me to a stop on the opposite street corner. I stand there, looking across four lanes of traffic at the tall Gothic doors, wide open on their hinges, and start to cry.

I cross the street with the light, thinking I'll just get a closer look at those doors, then duck in quickly because it's so terribly awkward to hang around on doorsteps. This is my signature move, that I make all accidents—even heart accidents—look intentional. A church service is already under way. Taking out my notebook, I keep telling myself that I'm here to study an anomaly, maybe to study this church. It seems different from what I remember church to be. Perhaps I'm looking for inspiration for a poem that I will write and take back to the poetry club at the bagel shop in Somerville.

But as usual, I am completely wrong about everything. My notebook page remains blank as I sit near the back, a whole pew to myself, and watch, like a starved person at a banquet, as a small community of Christians shares with one another confession, fellowship, and Communion.

My blank notebook is tucked back into my handbag and I'm waiting for the Red Line train outbound at Park Street, when I realize a woman from that congregation is standing on the center platform. Without thinking, I run up the stairs and down the other stairs and right up to her and ask, a bit breathlessly, if she doesn't mind talking to me until her train comes. I need a little perspective, I say. I have been nothing but critical of the religious establishment, for years, really. But I need a community, pretty much, umm . . . desperately. Can she tell me what she knows about that church?

Luckily for me, Stephanie is bemused rather than frightened. She is a post-doc student in the hard sciences at Harvard University and clearly an introverted personality, as, in my way, am I. But we instantly connect. If she thinks it's strange that I've started such an intense conversation with a total stranger, she doesn't mention it. We stand on a subway platform and talk about blind religion and imperfect churches and seeking for water in the desert for four or five or six long blessed minutes until both our trains come. I ride home feeling as if I might actually have made a friend.

The following Sunday I go to that church again. I have already decided to invite Stephanie over for dinner. This is nearly as impulsive a move as all the rest of my impulsive moves. I am a very nervous cook and usually will go to great lengths to avoid cooking for other people. But I'm desperate for human connection, post social networking. And there is inevitability to my realization that the alternative to screen time is table time. I plan a menu and buy a bottle of wine. I also go ahead and invite Nick, because he lives here.

On the evening of our dinner date, the land line phone rings and I pick it up. A computerized voice says to me, "You have a text message from—" and then Stephanie's voice says, "Stephanie." I think this is an excellent joke. I don't use computers to talk to other people, but what can I do when a computer calls me up and talks to me? The computer woman is telling me in her computer voice that Stephanie is still coming, but she's going to be late because she's at a talk at her school on the subject of Impostor Syndrome.

Two hours later Nick and Stephanie are both standing with wine glasses in our kitchen and I am making risotto for the first time. It isn't going as well for me as it did for the excellent cook I am trying to imitate. But I don't know if this is a problem with my technique or a problem with my attention, because I am utterly fascinated with the concept of Impostor Syndrome.

I press Stephanie to tell me all about it, and she says that her entire department was there, at this talk, but none of them had told each other they were going, and that seems to be pretty much the essence of Impostor Syndrome. It is the belief that you got into this Harvard University PhD program in the hard sciences somehow by accident, or by luck, or by some kind of dishonesty, because although it may appear to everybody else in the world that you are genuinely really good at what you do, you think you're just barely getting away with it. You think you're a fraud, an impostor.

I wonder—out loud—what we think it ought to feel like to be authentically good at something. What would it feel like to be authentically anything at all? Which leads me into a familiar rant about these latter days in which we all start using the self-checkout at the grocery and the do-it-yourself scanners that look like little guns.

I may be the only one who actually follows my weak but very dramatic thread, connecting Impostor Syndrome to a culture in which we all depend on electronic devices for constant validation. But it makes for a stimulating conversation and occasionally an all-out debate. On the second glass of wine, I get up the nerve to ask Stephanie again about God and the Bible and her experiences of being the progressive child of a conservative Christian faith, which is the rocky ground both of us have grown on. And then we spend another glass of wine debating whether Christianity and feminism can ever really work it out.

Just before she leaves, Stephanie asks me if I am on the Young Adults e-mail list at the church. I shake my head and smile and wait for her to hear what she just said.

"What," she says, "you don't consider yourself a young adult?"

"No, Stephanie," I reply, feeling a bit as if she has missed the context of the entire evening. "I am going for a year without the Internet. I don't have e-mail."

Instead of email I have snail mail, which is still baffling. My actor friend Jaysen, to whom I sent the homemade postcards, sends one back through the post right away. But by the time it arrives, a week has passed and I've forgotten about the entire thing. This is what snail mail is like. Where a conversation ought to be continuous, it isn't. There are gaps.

Among the black-marker triangles that I drew on the homemade postcard like a frame, Jaysen has nestled in purple script a quote by Anne Lamott: "Hope begins in the dark, the stubborn hope that if you just show up and try to do the right thing, the dawn will come."*

I hold the postcard and receive the rush of pleasure at the contact, but then I don't know what I should do next. How can I possibly reply back to this? With no "like" button and no re-tweet, how do I communicate resonance with this thought? Do I write a letter? If I write a letter, what do I write? And how long will that take? If I hear back, will I even remember what I wrote? By then will it matter? If not, does it matter now?

Life without Internet certainly does bring up a lot of questions.

Jacob has to call me to tell me I completely missed a special election in the state of Massachusetts. I hardly even knew about it, having been a bit preoccupied with this whole adventure of going for a year without the Internet, and not 100 percent solid on special elections in the first place. Jacob has to tell me that I missed it and that the result was an upset, and not in the direction I would have been expected to cast my vote.

This makes my heart hurt. It makes my heart hurt that just as I was learning to host a guest for dinner, I accidentally completely forgot to be civically involved, which is so much the opposite of what I hoped for from my year without the Internet. What also makes my heart hurt is that my niece, Beth, is staying with me for a

---

* Anne Lamott, *Bird by Bird: Some Instructions for Writing and Life* (New York: Anchor, 1995), *xxiii.*

couple of days, so I'm moping in the stupor of my loss while sitting in a room with somebody who can say, "I don't know who I would vote for. I don't know much about either one." Which makes me want to say back, "For goodness' sake, don't vote for their sparkling personalities. They're supposed to represent us, not be our friends. What do you want for your country? Who do you want us to be in the world?"

But then I get lost in this question too, because Beth and I are also talking about the earthquake in Haiti that killed 230,000 people and destroyed or damaged many, many buildings in the city of Port-au-Prince. Beth has someone in her life, someone who is close to her, whose family is in Haiti. She looks cold. "I don't know what to say, exactly," she says. "I don't feel it. I see the pictures. I hear the numbers. But I don't feel it."

I nod, and for a moment neither of us says anything at all. I haven't seen any images of the earthquake except in the newspaper, but I know exactly what she's talking about. I remember the footage of the Twin Towers coming down, when I was twenty-one years old, and I remember that horrible, empty, exhausted feeling, like "Is this it? Is this all I get?" I see the video armageddon and all the people screaming and dying and the flames, and all I feel is empty and alone?

Then the silence creeps up between us, Beth and me . . . with our twelve-year age difference spanning the birth of the digital generation. And I wonder what we think being authentically compassionate ought to feel like. I wonder what it would take for her and for me—over an election we didn't vote in and a shaking of the earth we didn't feel—to know beyond a doubt that we are human.

Beth is leaving Boston, going off to New York City and points beyond. Before she goes, I have asked her to babysit my two children so Nick and I can go on an outing with Jacob to Walden Pond, the place where the hermit philosopher Henry David Thoreau wrote that famous memoir that everybody assumes I have read, but I still haven't, called *Walden*.

Jacob says his favorite part in the book is about the ice cracking on the pond, and Kirsten Brandt in her last letter said the same thing, so it seems right that I should go to visit this famous pond in winter, under ice, and under a thick and gorgeous coating of fresh snow.

I drag my feet on the way out the door, and apart from my concern for Baby Stella, who can't be trusted to take a bottle, I know that if I could take the dining room window with me, I would. I prefer my snow to be on the other side of a window. Instead I bring my camera and stay behind the lens, photographing ice crystals from the very moment we get out of the car, even as Nick and Jacob begin to throw snowballs at each other. They laugh and duck behind trees. The whole thing seems a bit dangerous, or at least treacherously damp. But then I take pictures of them laughing, and then I take pictures of Nick's snowman that he builds at the end of the path, which is, like anything else Nick builds, a finish-quality creation. Finally, I sigh and tuck my camera under my coat and tromp around the lake to see the site of Thoreau's cabin, which is ten-by-fifteen feet and gives Jacob new perspective, he says, on the challenge of decorating his one-room studio apartment.

On the way back around the pond, I dip my hands into the snow and throw snow up into the air and watch it fall. With my camera still under my coat, I stand for a long moment with the sun low over the snow-covered trees. Jacob sees on his cell phone that he has missed a call from Beth, who says the baby is crying and won't take the bottle and are we coming home soon? Of course, a phone call like that ensures that we will be stuck in traffic in the tunnel for a long time, so I put my camera on a slow shutter speed and use the brake lights of the vehicle in front of us to draw neon hearts and letters in the air. When we get home, my baby is still crying, and Beth looks ashen and shaky. But I feel immensely ever so much better and, once again, absurdly grateful for the snow.

It is afternoon when I give Beth a ride to the train. On the way she and I talk about the phone, how she says she would much rather text than talk on the phone because, she says, she doesn't feel she's very good at listening. My son is hysterical with sadness as she leaves, and I can't help but think how funny it is that we make technology to solve these problems of distance and connection, of love and loss.

As dusk falls I watch Milo looking out the window saying, "Beth? Say good-bye? Cousin Beth? Say good-bye?" He becomes more and more distraught. And I know I will remember this day as the day my two-year-old grew a soul, as much as the soul can be understood to be that great yawning darkness that opens up in a human being like an insatiable wound—that great hole that now and forever will beg to be filled with meaning, with God, with art and theater and clicking around on the Internet, and with getting to say good-bye to your favorite grown-up cousin before she gets on the train.

The light is changing. The angle of the light is changing. Winter still seems forever. The ice is still thick and the wind is bitter cold as it comes in off the bay. But now there is light in the kitchen in the mornings. One day I am nursing Stella, sitting on the edge of Milo's bed, looking past the baby's fuzzy head through one doorway and another doorway into the sunlit kitchen, when I see a vision of myself being stitched together.

I find this picture quaint. I'm not quite sure why I keep repeating it back to myself, but I have grabbed on to this image and am holding on. It is the lottery for which I have bought this ticket. It is that sticking phrase by Eugene O'Neill, which floats all over the Internet, ironically pulled out of context from a controversial play that hardly anybody ever reads: "Man is born broken. He lives by mending. The grace of God is glue."*

I think I could almost believe in this, this mending grace.

---

* Eugene O'Neill, *The Great God Brown: Classic Drama* (SquareSpace Independent Publishing Platform, ttps://www.squarespace.com/, 2014), 66.

Three

Kitchen Ghosts

I have a lot of healing to do in the kitchen. I encounter it the way I seem to encounter everything else, full speed ahead and not realizing where I'm going. I am already deep into becoming Suzy Homemaker, who excels in this new-to-me role as keeper of the home, before I remember that I am an eating disorder survivor. I am among the kitchen wounded, the kitchen disabled. In kitchens, I can't use all my limbs.

It's a strange irony that I am quite so bad at cooking, since the mother who bore me was famous for teaching hundreds of thousands of people skills for food self-sufficiency. Her name was Carla Emery, and her legacy was a cookbook, which is not only a cookbook. *The Encyclopedia of Country Living*, now in a 40th anniversary edition, is a five-pound, 800-page manual of how to feed a family from the land. It influenced the 1970s back-to-the-land movement and has helped to propel the modern homesteading movement ever since.

My mother's book is a legend. Her life was a force. This is true. It is also true that her youngest daughter couldn't learn from her how to cook or how to feed herself.

Carla Emery died five years ago, suddenly, of septicemia associated with low blood pressure. But long before my mother died, I threw myself in the opposite direction from everything she stood for. In the same year that Y2K failed utterly to destroy civilization as we knew it, I left my birth state of Idaho for California, leaving the agrarian culture to hit the biggest cities I could find. I put my mother's book out of sight and planted myself in concrete, as she, in a zigzag path across the country, continued to preach the gospel of self-reliance. I wore mascara and strappy sandals and didn't keep house plants and said I would always be a career woman. And I never, ever, ever learned to cook.

When I have dinners with Jacob, Jacob cooks. When Nick is home, Nick cooks. When neither of them is here, I eat canned soup and toast with my two-year-old, and that's just the way it is. That's the best I can do. Although no one ever wanted it this way, my food resistance long ago developed into food disorder, manifesting as more than a decade of disordered eating and food-related anxiety.

Now here I am, a stay-at-home mom with no Internet, tying a striped apron around my waist. In the fridge, I meet myself as a bulimic teenager, binging and purging as an obvious response to the stress that was my daily bread. In the cupboards I meet my family history, of arms elbow deep in dough and sleeves rolled up to milk the cow and churn the butter. And every time I make a pot of coffee, I meet my grief for the career I fought so hard for and then lost.

From a historian's view, I was a minor figure, only a moderate success. But I was young and female in a highly competitive field, and I was rising. In my last full year of directing plays, the city newspaper published a list of the ten best theater productions of the year, and three of them were mine. I left my baby with a babysitter, wore fancy dresses, and gave speeches to accept awards. The features and the good reviews filled up a folder in my hope chest. One critic called me "wunderkind."

I did love the accolades, but I also truly loved the work. I felt that theater people were my family and that telling stories well was the most important thing a person could ever do. I didn't feel it happening when my speed kicked up so high that I was no longer grounded. I didn't feel it happening when I became inauthentic, or deceitful, or when my husband and I completely lost touch with each other. I didn't feel it happening when I lost my own moral compass. I didn't know, and still don't know, quite what to blame.

My last rehearsal ever as a stage director was a sunny winter day in California. I was five months pregnant with Stella. The show was close to opening and not in good shape. The biggest problem was with the scenery design, being done by my husband, though my own work wasn't much better. It was early January. In October, I had moved into my friend Missy's spare room and Nick had retained a divorce lawyer. In November, I had been pulled over on a California freeway going 113 miles an hour and had made the move back into my own house. We both were still reeling with the betrayal and the shock. I was muscling through life for the sake of my one-year-old son and unborn daughter.

That day we were doing a run-through of the entire play. After the run-through, it would be my job to hear notes from the artistic director, take the ones that were for me, and pass on all the rest. I spent the entire run preparing for what I knew was coming. The artistic director would have criticism for the scenic designer, still (barely) my husband, and I was going to have to be the bearer of bad news. I thought I might shatter from the pressure. Just before the moment came for me to receive my notes, I left.

It was sunny in the parking lot, I remember. The sky was blue. The world was surprisingly not broken. I thought if I could just get a day or so to get my head on straight, I could come back and I could fix it—the show, at least—I wasn't sure about the rest. But they didn't want me to come back. I was fired over the phone as I sat in a medical clinic helping my toddler do puzzles, waiting for a second trimester prenatal exam.

That was the beginning of the end of my career, but nowhere near the end of the losses. I lost two more jobs related to this new problem with my reputation, since I walked out on an artistic director, then two more because they were too close to the day my second child would be born. At the same time, my circle of friends was altering in the most dramatic ways. Few saw me as a real woman, a real person desperately in need of companionship and compassion and help. Most still saw me as I had wanted to be seen, a ruthless and ambitious theater star who didn't need any help from anyone. The crowd that had existed around me as I moved through work spaces and accomplishments and celebrations vanished into air.

In the spring, my first daughter was born, and I fell headlong into the challenge of caring for two babies. It was a wilder, busier schedule than I had ever experienced, even in all my ambitious workaholic life. The calendar pages turned without my having given them permission to turn. Before I knew it, a half a year had passed without my having earned any money of my own. Nick got a better job, with benefits, at the opposite end of the country, and we drained my personal bank account to travel two thousand miles in two cars away from all my professional contacts and creative friends.

I survived the change. But I sure didn't like it. I didn't like feeling that I didn't have any purpose in life, and then have my husband get all grumpy with me because he thought surely taking care of our amazing children qualifies as a purpose for my life. I didn't like feeling jealous of women on the other side of the gap, including my once-friends back in California, who still do what I used to do and do it well. Most of all, I didn't like the feeling that I had failed.

All this history seems to live strongest in my kitchen. The ghosts of my past selves interrupt me and distract, even when I'm doing something so simple as boiling water. But my husband isn't home, and I am. I read and re-read his recipes, struggle to get the bread to rise, and write things like "good cranberry muffins" and "lentil soup" on each page of the cornflower blue notebook.

Maybe it's because the gaps in my heart are so raw and dripping blood, or because my need for healing is so urgent, but I march up to the pastor of the beautiful, grand church in the Back Bay and ask if I can be baptized. I don't have much of an idea of what I'm doing. I'm still a little cynical at heart, not sure what I believe, if anything. But I seem to have a hope for a healing, stitching-back-together grace. And I have no other way, no other hope to turn to.

I am invited to the new members class, where I promise the pastor and two other couples, all established Christians moving over from different churches, that I am not really new to the Christian faith. Jesus was a pulse in my mother's blood, and her blood runs in me. I was raised with faith and even read the whole Bible once, every single word, when I was a teenager.

In a room full of generally progressive social-justice-minded Christians, it is safe for me to admit that when I read the Bible at that time, I mostly hated it. The offense had been personal. As a young teenager I had read feminism and cared deeply about human rights. I was passionate about the unique problems of women, both in the United States and in other countries. I read Alice Walker and Nawal El Sadaawi and wrote my high school senior thesis on the complexities of Western intervention in the problem of female genital mutilation.

I hated the church of my childhood because I heard them say outright that they hated feminism. I heard them say that God had made it this way, that men were the heads of households, and though men weren't perfect, women still weren't to interfere. This kind of research that I was doing was dangerous, not my business. These were issues I should leave in the hands of godly men. My gifts were utterly and totally rejected, and I retaliated.

I read the Bible then, beyond the familiarity I had from Sunday school, largely for the purpose of argument. It was the beginning of years of openly disputing the Christian faith. I married a man who was an established atheist, and I tucked away whatever was left of my faith, deep inside the argument. I built a little brick wall around it and moved on with my life. But as I tell it to the pastor, my faith itself—my belief in good and God and Christ resurrected—has always been there, always held tender and close to my heart. It wasn't broken by something as weak as human anger. And it doesn't want to stay inside that old brick wall anymore.

My story is met in the new members class with welcome and understanding, and even a bit, I think, of gratitude. But of course I am a storyteller, and the version I have told them is a bit more polished than the broken truth. The truth is I am brokenhearted. The truth is that Jesus appears to the brokenhearted. He is precisely the key that fits that lock. I have read in one of my poetry books that there is a church in Iran with the following inscription, carved in stone over its door, written by the thirteenth-century Sufi poet Rumi:

> *Where Jesus lives, the great-hearted gather.*
> *We are a door that's never locked.*
> *If you are suffering any kind of pain,*
> *stay near this door. Open it.**

---

*Jalal al-Din Rumi, *The Essential Rumi, New Expanded Edition*, trans. Coleman Barks (New York: HarperOne, 2004), 201.

I have no more confidence than I ever did in Christian culture. I'm not very confident of my theology, and I don't have a solid experience of conversion. But stronger than all these questions is the promise—from all the things I learned as a child and all the things I read in the Bible with my most critical eye—the promise of forgiveness. And in the gospel is a promise of rest. I am reaching out for these promises because I have no other choices. I have no other doors to try. I come empty-handed.

And this is what I love best about our big, loving, beautiful, expansive God. He will take me any way I'll come: even with my snark, my cynicism, my impulsiveness, my anger and old hurts. Later I will say that my conversion is proof of only one true thing, and that's the length of God's arm.

My brother doesn't have any idea what I'm talking about. Jacob has taken the secular path even more securely than I did, perhaps never feeling the pull to God that I have always felt. He is supportive, though, as good siblings are, and he finds it particularly defensible that I am seeking out community, since I am going through this time without the Internet. He sees in the church a kind of ready-made social group, arranged around what he might describe as my subject of interest.

I adore my brother, my brilliant, intellectual brother. We have a fascinating and still very enjoyable conversation about it all, and I will continue to process my life and my faith through him, because that's just the way things are. But I understand that he doesn't understand.

My husband is something different. Nick doesn't care a bit about the church and prefers that I don't invite him to come along. But Nick understands me. He understands what faith can do for me and my broken heart. That's why he keeps encouraging me to go every Sunday morning. He makes pancakes for the babies and changes their diapers and drives the five blocks through bitter, icy wind to the Metro station, where I take the subway train alone into the heart of the city.

He says that when I come home from church, I'm calmer. He says I'm more myself: less wounded and less scared.

I get baptized on Valentine's Day. Jacob comes along to see the occasion and so does Nick, who stands in the back in his good coat holding Stella and Milo and looking inordinately proud for an atheist. The pastor blesses me and leads the congregation in prayer for me, and in a move that she and I discussed beforehand, she baptizes me in the name of God, "Mother of us all." Which makes the so-often rejected feminist in me cry and seize, with sheer gratitude, the miracle of welcome.

Here is the promise, remembered from a child's story and now enfleshed, of unconditional welcome and expansive, limitless forgiveness. I catch a thread of it, just a thread. In this place, faith is not a hard shell of a thing. It is a movement. It is a direction. It is the magic stuff in which all the dead broken-off ends of things are trying to reach out to one another to get healed.

The next day I have a postcard in the mailbox from the wonderful actor mystic Jaysen, who puts inspirational quotes in stars and hearts on my pre-stamped postcards. Today around a star that Milo and I scrawled in red marker, he has drawn a sea of little green ink hearts. On the inside of the star, in all caps, is one word: "SHINE."

The pace of our house is dropping down, down from the head-long rush, into a settled kind of rest. When I finish writing letters in the evenings, Nick takes off his headphones and looks at me expectantly. He thinks I'll come hang out with him on the couch, which I will, just as soon as I have a blanket and a cup of tea. Romance likes the stillness. Romance likes the gaps.

There are more moments of connection between us lately. More often I smile at him when he comes in the door from his long, long workdays. More often I miss him when he's gone. More often we actually communicate things that we're thinking or hand off parenting or housekeeping tasks with some quality other than fierce resentment.

He is a little more settled in his new job at American Repertory Theater, and though he still rarely gets a full weekend off, he is less absorbed in it, more able to give attention to me and to his kids, and to let me have precious downtime where he can watch the kids and I can have a few hours to get my head clear.

This is how it is possible for me to get away to the library on Saturday morning. All these changes have put me in the mode of introspection. And with the seismic shifts of these two months—in faith, in politics, in food—I feel I need to relearn the entire world, starting from the beginning. I want to try again. So many things I've gotten wrong.

I pack on my winter gear and shoulder a book bag full of empty notebooks. But at the door Nick stops me with his best authoritarian voice: "You stay away from those computers, you hear?"

I roll my eyes. That little Google incident, where I erased my profile comment, was so totally two months ago. I'm different now.

Apparently, so is my husband. When I first told him my plan to go for a year without the Internet, he said, "You're trying to live in 1980 for some reason." Now he seems to like 1980 well enough. I cook. I spend less money. I notice when he comes home from work. And, since we're not both trying to finish reading the Internet every night, we go to bed earlier, and together, which comes with certain advantages.

Less Internet, more sex. Who knew?

Perhaps because we're spending so much time on it, Nick has suddenly found unacceptable the wilting mattress that we bought used for our first apartment nearly ten years ago. He has arranged to bring home quite the upgrade, the royal mattress belonging to the same Lady Macbeth who once haunted my hallway, the anti-heroine of the bloody Shakespearean tragedy in which a power couple murder every single soul who is between them and the Scottish throne. The show has closed, the set is being dismantled, and the mattress is in fine condition, as long as you don't mind sleeping on a little dried stage blood.

This is a thing that Nick and I have always shared, besides theater and heartbreak and trying to be funny even when life isn't funny. We both love to live a thrifty, handmade life. Nick calls it "interrupting the waste stream," and it is his hobby. He likes it best to take an ugly thing and make it beautiful again. But he likes it very, very best to drag home some nearly dead, resurrected treasure and lay it at my feet and have me love it. He speaks to me in this language instead of in words. He always has.

Today his salvaged gift to me is the luxury of Lady Macbeth's royal queen-sized mattress. He brings it home after dark, pulling it off the truck by himself with his long arms like a wingspan.

We haven't seen my brother Dan since we all gathered at our house for Christmas. Nick's schedule is still tight, so we decide to make a trip to New York City in one long day. We leave very early in the morning, driving the four hours south ahead of the traffic.

As always, I lighten and soften in the presence of my family. Dan plays the guitar, and we talk about self-improvement, which is a passion we both share, and I chat with his wife, Miriam, in the kitchen about the difference between reading on the Internet and reading books.

The kids have a fabulous and wild time with their three older cousins, and when we all decide to go to the library late in the afternoon and both of our kids fall asleep in the car, Nick and I are ready to let it slide. We buy expensive lattes in paper cups and park on the side of the road and watch the shadow climb the cliff on the bank of the Hudson River.

I don't listen to the radio in the car anymore, since I've become an acolyte of the silence, so I am already irritated by the murmuring noise in the background when Nick hears something that captures his attention and turns up the volume. The golf star Tiger Woods has cheated on his wife. He's having a press conference to tell the whole world about his feelings, and the whole world appears to feel like listening. I fold my arms across my chest and look hard out the passenger-side window until the celebrity has finished apologizing to his fans, and Nick turns off the radio with a click.

"How did he do?" I ask.

"Not well."

"What do you think he should have said? What would have been better?"

"Nothing," he answers. "Absolutely nothing."

We look out again on the view of the river and the cliff and the slowly darkening sky, but we both know our thoughts are no longer able to receive the peace. We have bumped into the wound, long scarred over, but still bleeding underneath. And I don't know if I have enough of a wall left anymore to keep it in.

When we get back to my brother's house, they have another dinner guest. Her name is Amy, and the kids know her as an aunt. As the grown-ups eat dinner and talk the way grown-ups do, nine-year-old Elijah wolfs his food and tries to bolt. When his mother asks him to be polite and stick around, Amy presents a discussion topic. The Navy has just revised its rule about women serving on submarines. What does Elijah think of that? Should women be allowed to serve in the military the same as men?

Elijah brightens up. He is interested in this, as he is interested in most anything related to the military. He thinks it's okay for women to be in the armed forces, including combat, except if there is a baby at home who needs milk, because it is better for babies to have that milk, and that is something only women can do.

His dad, who is, just to be clear, my brother, agrees. "It is a greater hardship," he says, "for a baby to go without its mother than its father."

I have a deep and clunky feeling that it's a bit more complicated than that, but I can't get into it right now because I am too busy trying to keep my two-year-old out of the art supplies and my crawling, cruising baby off the stairs. Someone else says, "That depends on the individuals involved," which I appreciate. But I am still thinking of what exactly it is that I want to add when the conversation moves on without me. All I can do is lean down over Stella as she crawls up the bottom stair of the wide wooden staircase, over and over and over again, and dread to think of how young Elijah might enforce his rule.

We leave right after dinner so the kids will sleep on the way home, and we are somewhere in the middle of Connecticut when Nick says, "I don't think I would have been a very healthy stay-at-home dad."

"Why is that?" I ask.

"I don't last very long at it," he answers. "I'm not as calm as you are. I start to crave alone time. I can't go very long before I crave alone time."

I turn to him in slow motion. I feel myself hurtling toward my feminist roots at the speed of rock-and-roll angst, grasping for some shred of teenage Riot Grrl solidarity.

"Do you think it's just an accident?" I sputter. "That it's just a matter of what, my personality? That I'm somehow naturally suited to, to what . . . ? Service?"

Nick's eyes stare fixedly ahead. The stone face has snapped back into place. I turn to my right, where the great frozen forests of New England are rushing by.

I know he didn't mean to say that my former career was wrong for me. I know he didn't mean to dismiss my gifts or disregard my current struggles, even as I bend like a pretzel to fit myself into this different space of life. But his refusal to acknowledge my struggle is his refusal to acknowledge me. My husband has never yet given me credit for the loss I voluntarily took or the pain it caused me. He may well see me all these evenings I spend learning to cook for his children while he does the work we once did side by side. But he has never yet spoken words that do it justice. I don't think he knows how.

In the second month of Stella's newborn life, I cried every day. The babies were just too much for me, the two of them, a newborn and a toddler, doing bedtime by myself, with my husband working long hours and my big sister and my mother-in-law both gone back on airplanes to their faraway homes. Every night I cried, with one or the other or both of those babies screaming at me, like tiny furies, fully human and so, so much in need. There was just more need than there was me.

I cried because I couldn't do it. But I also cried because my ego was disappearing. I was losing self in little bits, like fingers, and I knew even then the change was irreversible. Now, yes, I am calm when they scream at me. Now, yes, I get along without so much alone time. Now, yes, my own needs don't rank so high in the pantheon of household gods. You can call that magic if you want, but it is a real and painful magic, neither sudden nor inexplicable.

I do not for one moment regret that crucible. In diapers and tears I began to value my achievement less and my compassion more. Something precious and true began to enmesh itself where the ego was uprooted, and not for all the oil in Arabia would I unravel its fledgling weave. But why was it only me? Why didn't something like this happen to my husband?

Tonight, as I take the wheel for the last and midnight hour of the drive, I know that the man in my life has never seen those rocks. Between him and the bottom there is a safety net. It is inarticulate, invisible, yielding and unyielding, like a chain. Between my husband and the hard place, there is me. And as much as I grieve the beating I took, I'm also glad I could be there. I'm glad I was.

In the morning, long before I've had a full night's rest, I hear my baby daughter in the next room wake up crying, and I remember the day that she was born, out of me, in a miracle that justifies the very name of God. I walk with her into the kitchen, right past the striped apron, and I think the role of homemaker deserves some reclaiming. I want to be a whole person, capable of income earning, but also capable of feeding myself. I want to be a whole person, capable of humility as well as leadership. And I have everything I need to become whole in this way if I can only drop the force of my own resistance. I have everything I need to lay to rest the kitchen ghosts.

I spend the last week of February baking bread, and reading old books, and scribbling in my notebooks, and looking out the windows at the relentlessly unappealing outdoor weather, which seems like it will never break.

I'm so absorbed in my thoughts and all the ghosts I've raised that I forget we have scheduled another dinner party. Sarah and Ian are another couple from church, younger than we are, with two careers and no kids. They are working on buying a house in the suburbs. All this is intimidating enough, so it's good that I don't find out until they arrive that they are also both Italian-American and Sarah is a food blogger. She is someone who blogs. About food. This makes them a bit of an intimidating crowd to cook for, and all the more so since right at that very moment I am using an actual hammer—I couldn't find the right kitchen tool so I dipped into Nick's toolbox—to break up what is essentially an overcooked pizza crust into a completely self-invented homemade appetizer.

I slip the hammer behind my apron and back toward the toolbox. For a moment I think if we're going to make a habit of inviting near strangers over for dinner, we should install a trapdoor so that I can have someplace to disappear to. But our adorable children break the moment and, of course, it's easier than that. Turns out my broken-up bits of oily pizza crust are very good, especially with a good salsa. And who cares anyway? The food is a vehicle. It's a good thing, and sometimes even a wonderful thing, but it's also just a thing we all need on the way to being human.

Sarah and Ian and Nick and I talk and laugh and raise glasses of wine together, and though we come from different places, the air over our table is rich in oxygen and room. They tell us at the end that our food was very good, and I don't think they're lying. In fact, I think Ian would take twice as many of Nick's peanut butter cookies if he thought anyone else would do the same.

I did not intend to become a homemaker. As marriage was to Juliet, it was an honor that I dreamt not of. But it happened. Like a failed dish at a dinner party, it happened. And it lived on with dialogue and forgiveness. It lived on with something the Christians call grace, which is like a vision in a sunlit kitchen, of a woman being stitched together into something whole.

PART TWO

the *Rain*

Four

Walden

I'm cooking every night now, like a little storm in the kitchen. Hunger unleashed. The house fills up with smells from rising bread and simmering pots. I talk on the phone with my brother, who tells me how he remembers watching our mother making soups. How she would take something out of the fridge, look at it, smell it . . . and toss it in. He makes her sound a little undomesticated, a little wild. I wish I knew.

My family has a story. Long ago and far away, the story goes, we lived a different kind of life. We were at the center of an entire movement to live a different kind of life. I have only glimpses of it. Flashes. The orchard and the swinging bridge. Apple plum butter. Rattlesnakes and guns. My sisters rode horses. My father used equipment that I can neither name nor accurately describe to help the neighbors put up hay.

My mother was born a farm girl in Montana, just ahead of the baby boom. She was a natural leader, born to teach. The way she tells it, she saw all the hippies showing up in rural places with no skills, and she decided somebody needed to help them. She started making a manual of skills for rural living. She called it *The Old-Fashioned Recipe Book*. At first she published it herself. It was mimeographed, and each chapter was a different color. Every page was practical instruction in some half-forgotten skill. The whole thing was a gift from my mother, right from her heart, to help any yearning soul to achieve the goal of a life lived closer to the land.

She hit a nerve. Or maybe the nerve hit her. She had a practical manual for living off the land, and when she took it to a Seattle craft fair in 1974, her table was mobbed. It was a quick road to celebrity, although a short one. She took her books on the road and sold them at fairs all over the country. People admired her and wanted to hear her speak. She did TV and radio. She took animals with her on her tour and took them on TV with her. She milked a goat on late-night television, and America thought it was hysterical.

In those days, the whole nation was singing with my mother this song of going back to the land. It was a song of a simpler life, agrarian values, and a sacred connection with the earth that bears our food: a lifestyle that to most was deeply unfamiliar and yet, also, so much like coming home.

But that era of the '70s didn't last, and I was born too late to see it. I have no way to split the family legends from the facts. I wasn't there. I am the elder child of the Millennials, the leading edge of the Digital Generation. I missed the whole darn thing.

I pull out the entire crisper drawer from my fridge and set it on the table. Celery. Onions. Squash. A cabbage too. I cut everything up. Everything. I drop it into my soup and watch it boil.

I still am tracking my accomplishments in the cornflower blue notebook, though it seems more and more ridiculous as I write in things like "made up an original recipe for crackers, too salty" and "mom soup." The most sane-looking page is where I write the dozens of book titles I've completed, which is actually a bit impressive, and where I write how many chapters I've completed in the Bible.

I am reading the entire Bible. My personality hasn't changed a bit, even after all these transformations, which means I am reading the entire Bible on a strict and quite ambitious schedule. I expect to finish it in July.

I am reading the Bible backward. Jacob encourages this, comparing me to the clerics of the Medieval ages, who he says would have read backward into the Hebrew Bible, mapping out the signs and omens of the coming Christ. He is glad for the gesture of free thinking, I think, like a final holdout against the grain of Christian culture. But for me it is more like holding a great painting upside down. I need to know what the Bible actually says, not what I think it says. I need it to say something different to me than what it said before.

The last time I read the Bible all the way through, I had just turned fifteen. I was on the road with my mother, tagging along with her on her strange itinerant path along the fringes of America. I was making a decision then, a very hard decision, about which way to walk, standing in this rift between my mother's way and everybody else's way and deciding which side of the canyon I would claim as mine. My mother's charismatic Christian faith was passionate, but also innocent. So many things—so many hard things—she just chose not to see. I read the Bible back then and marked it up with red pen, highlighting all the dark passages, all the violent ones, all the passages I took as proof that my naive and idealistic mother was blind.

It is the experiment of going off the Internet that makes my faith reversal possible. I give it full credit, 100 percent credit. This is not because I think the Internet prefers one faith tradition over another, or that there is some shield against Jesus somehow embedded in my handheld phone. It is this: social networking is a natural enemy to humility. Certain kinds of changes are hard to make when you're performing your identity for the appreciation of a crowd. And on the Internet are still the bones of my old selves: I, who spent much time criticizing the weaknesses of the Christian faith; I, who spent so much time trying to tell believers they were blind. How is it that now I turn again and beg for healing?

My network and close family is made up almost entirely of atheists. Later, when all this comes out, people will say things like "You don't really believe that, do you?" and "Are you sure it isn't a cult?" They'll also recommend that I read the notorious atheist Richard Dawkins. But by the grace of God, at the nascent budding of my grown-up faith, they have absolutely no idea what I am up to. With neither Foursquare nor Facebook to track where I am sitting Sunday mornings, I worship in the blessed anonymity of the unplugged. And none but God knows how extreme my reversal really is.

If I were asked why I go to church, I would say something like this: I go to church because big churches make me cry, and here in Boston there are these great big churches all over the place, and I am afraid I will be taken at a stoplight one day by an uncontrollable episode of crying. Then I'll run a red light, and probably hurt somebody, maybe seriously, and in that scenario I really could never forgive myself.

In other words, I go to church for the same reason that I imagine anybody goes to church, which is that I am compelled and have lost the power to resist.

In December, before the snow came, I thought it was possible to avoid being alone with myself. Now that seems ridiculous. Now I am alone with myself all the time, sometimes for hours at a time. In all those gaps grows a craving for the sacred, a wind that builds on itself like cataclysmic weather. The more it is satisfied, the more it grows. And so I read the Bible, like food for a hungry person, like Braille to the blind, starting with the end of the world and working backward toward creation.

The Bible isn't the only thing I'm reading. Books are everywhere in our little apartment. There are books in the kitchen, books in the living room, books in a tall stack on my desk until it falls over and scares the cat. I am reading cookbooks. I am reading parenting books. I am reading a hardback called *The Call of Solitude*. I am also reading *Lemony Snicket's Unfortunate Series of Events*.

All our books come from the thrift store. We go on Tuesdays. It has replaced the library. I have a luminous and dreamlike state reserved for this one magic hour in my week, when Milo sits up in the used furniture section, with his feet sticking out over the edge of a green-tinged golden easy chair that never sells, poring over dusty and discarded children's books like sacred tomes. Stella slumps slightly in the mismatched shopping cart, gurgling into her sippy cup. And I scan box after box and shelf after shelf of dusty worlds, searching for treasure.

One day at the Goodwill I find three copies of *Walden*, the famous opt out memoir by Thoreau, all three in different printings. I buy them all. I have no confidence in my attention span, although God blesses my enthusiasm. My plan is to switch back and forth between the different printings of this brainy book to help keep myself focused. But I am not even through the first long chapter before I come to realize that this is not just any book of philosophy. Henry David Thoreau is not just any philosopher. He is *my* philosopher. He belongs to me, *personally*. He speaks the cry of my own inarticulate breast.

I have a photo that I took of the sign at the site of Thoreau's cabin, capped with new snow on the day that Jacob took us out to Walden Pond. It bears a famous quote from his writing, famous enough to be recognized even by some of us who hadn't actually read that, which says,

> I went into the woods because I wished to live deliberately, to
> front only the essential facts of life, and see if I could not learn

what it had to teach, and not, when I came to die, discover that I had not lived.*

I put the photo on my desktop. These words will inspire me. "We are alike, Thoreau and I," I write, in longhand, in one of my chatty letters. "We are both hermits."

Sadly, our love affair, as all love affairs with dead philosophers must, comes to a bitter end. First, I become frustrated because he knows so darn much about nature. Here is Thoreau, communing with the cycle of the seasons, while all I can do is watch the squirrels dig stale Christmas candy out of my trash cans. Here is Thoreau, calling all the plants and animals by name, and also by genus, which is clearly just for showing off, while I can't even name the shrubs along the waterfront. For him, the hermit's discipline of silence is a test of his integration with his world. But I am not integrated with my world at all. I am free floating, like a lost puzzle piece. I look at the trees and the sky and hear nothing but the vast intimidating silence.

I go back to the library, thinking that I might find some books to fill in all these great holes in my knowledge. But it doesn't take, partly because I am distracted by my kids—Stella doesn't stay in the carrier very long anymore—but mostly because I am overwhelmed by the sheer mass of information. I stumble away from what is literally an entire aisle of books about natural things, none of which seems to connect particularly with me. While Thoreau continues to wax romantic over weeds, I think of the poverty I felt when I shut off the bottomless well of images in my computer screen. I thought at first that the world itself was bare of pictures. What a strange thing that seems now, for any person, to think.

But oh, how different everything was for him!—for the bachelor hunter-fisher-farmer—to take his turn toward Eden in the bosom of

---

* Henry David Thoreau, *Walden: Or, Life in the Woods* (New York: Dover, 1995), 59.

his very own native woods! How different that was from this that I have chosen: my self-imposed imprisonment in the half-and-half jungle of Quincy, Mass., where nothing is fully domesticated and nothing is wild.

We live only one block from the bay. On weekdays I run to the beach in the early morning, before Nick goes to work, and do a brief but satisfying bit of yoga with the dawn over the quiet fringe of the Atlantic Ocean. The image is stunning. It's absurd, how orange the sky is, how audaciously Not Blue the sky is, as if it didn't go to school the day we all learned to write, "The sky is blue," one hundred times per page in our composition books. Has this always been here? All this beauty? So close to me? That all I had to do was walk out the door and look?

To get to the beach I have to cross a highway, what at this end of the country people call a parkway. One still cold morning I pause to wait for a break in the traffic and see beside me a tree that is brambly and viney and small. Without knowing how I know it, I know that this tree will flower. I know it will. I'm sure of it. And I am relieved, because now I know that even in my twenty-first-century ignorance, I can't miss the spring completely. I will watch the spring happen on this tree.

By the time I've walked the one long block back to my house, my intuition has been forcibly evolved into a project. I will commit to a tree. I will watch that tree. I will photograph it. I will capture its change. In this way, I will know the beautiful, cataclysmic transformation that was so loved by the naturalist philosopher of Walden Pond. Whatever it is that he felt, I will feel it too.

I pick a tree that is convenient, one that I pass by every time I leave, in any direction. It is a profoundly average tree, but I convince myself this is the best choice. I am looking for an absolutely authentic experience of spring, and I don't want to work with any outliers.

I creep in closer to get a better look, hoping that the people who own this yard are superbly understanding or, better yet, not at home. When I see and touch the twigs, I discover that the tree isn't dead or even asleep. It has already begun, the spring. I missed it! There are all these little popcorn kernels on the twigs, unopened buds of something. I envision that each little popcorn kernel bud will unfurl itself into a leaf. I want to watch it happen. I might drive by again later today. I don't want to miss the first one.

But I don't get back to my tree that day because life happens. When I finally do get back, early the next morning, I am relieved. I didn't miss anything. The buds have not begun to open. I go back the next day, and the next, and again the buds have not begun to open. The next day, and the next, the buds still have not begun to open.

At this point I wonder, briefly, and with all due respect, if I picked a bad tree. Maybe this one is broken. Maybe those kernel-looking things have been there all winter and aren't a sign of spring. I start flirting with other trees. I'm not picky anymore. I'll look at any tree. Is there anything changing out here? I scan the bare branches for buds, looking for the secret beginnings of things. And I do see things. I see buds. But I never see them appear. And I never see them change.

Of course, in my logical brain I know exactly why this is happening. I never see things change because I log all my data in a freeze frame, always glancing over on my way to something else. Suddenly this is everything I want to change about myself. This is exactly why I feel so broken. I dream a magic needle that could sew the pieces back together. From freeze frames into filmstrip into living world, I could stitch myself back together to the trees.

If I have any hope that this is possible, that is because I can feel it happening in books and also in letters. The thoughts get stuck together bit by bit, like a pie crust, out of tweet-able bits into longer and longer sections of real life. I do still love the postcards I get from Jaysen, with their one-line quotables and pretty line drawings. But I crave even more deeply the long handwritten letters I get from Nick's grandmother, Evelyn, my first real pen pal, who sends me stationery-store envelopes marked with her loopy, slanted cursive. Equally precious are the letters I get from Amy, my crunchy friend back in California, who has hair like a mountainside and puts essences of things in little bottles. I sit down and write her a long letter about my tree. She sends me back a poem she wrote about a train.

We're getting ready for a visit from my mother-in-law, Bernie, my children's only living grandmother. Since I walked off my daily cute-kid picture-posting duties on Facebook, I've made a point of calling her once a week and writing down the funny things our very verbal toddler says to make her smile.

I have to pick her up from the airport with no cell phone and no ability to text, but I make the best of it by convincing my son that the long walk across the sky bridge from the parking garage will be an educational adventure. Milo does indeed have an adventure, "seeing the airplanes," and I have Stella safe in the wrap on my chest, but at the sight of my mother-in-law, I blanch. I have seen her oxygen tube before, tucked under her nose and behind her ears, running back to a canister that she can carry in a bag or drag in her rolling luggage. I have heard, in our weekly phone calls, that she is now wearing that oxygen all the time. But I was not prepared for this, that my husband's mother, in the half a year since we last saw her, has grown suddenly old.

I worry that my children will be alarmed, but they don't care. I am the one who stares too long at the color of her skin and startles at the shallowness of her breath. I am the one who suddenly regrets everything there is to regret about my stupid experiment, that I am handling my kids instead of carrying her bags, that I didn't bend my stupid principles enough to use Google Earth to research the airport, that I didn't just carry a cell phone and pick her up at the curb like a civilized person.

We all struggle with the long walk back across the sky bridge, but Bernie is happy. She is happy that Milo knows her, that he calls her "Grandma." She tells him that she has brought him lots of books. I have to help her get her seatbelt on because her arm is too weak. This makes me feel suddenly horrified, as if I'm about to be the only grown-up in this situation, and that's a very, very bad thing, as I'm still the kind of person who would go for a year without the Internet. Which is, clearly, not a very grown-up thing to do.

Nick isn't able to make it home in time for dinner. Although this is normal, on this day I find it completely unacceptable. I want him to come home right this second and pamper his mother beyond all reason. I adore my mother-in-law. I met her when she was young, as Nick and I started dating quite young, and at a time when my own mother and I were not on speaking terms. She and I connected on a dozen things. We both had worked in nursing homes, we both were addicted to smoking cigarettes, we both enjoyed snarky political digs, and we both were crazy about Nick. It was the cigarettes, probably, that made the strongest bond. At family gatherings, it always put us together, at the edges, indulging our bad habit in places where nobody else wanted to be.

Nick's mother tells me now that she thinks she has finally done it. She has finally quit smoking. She had meant for it to be a surprise, for her sons, after many attempts and many failures. But she grimaces; she isn't supposed to have it near the oxygen. She explains that her blood-oxygen levels are low, but the doctors can't tell her exactly why. It isn't emphysema. I feel suddenly frightened, and I have nothing to add. All I can do is put away our ashtray, which we have kept for the sole purpose of her visits. I quit smoking years ago, before I had kids.

Nick still is not home when we settle in for the night. Bernie sleeps with a breathing machine that fills our little apartment with the sound of whirring. Hours later I watch as Nick comes home from work and pauses, silently, still in his coat, at the end of the couch, and stares at his mom sleeping behind her mask.

In the morning Bernie watches the kids so Nick and I can do a long errand to the Registry of Motor Vehicles, to get our in-state drivers' licenses. The waiting room puts me into a mild state of shock. The trouble is not the sheer number of people, or even the overwhelming mass of bureaucratic infrastructure. It is simply the television screens, hanging over our heads where trees ought to be. I have not seen changing, moving pictures since November.

I take out my scrap of paper and start writing things down. Top ten movies by box-office receipts. I had never heard of any of them. Top ten iTunes downloads. I had never heard of any of them. Celebrity photos by the paparazzi. I really don't know who any of these people are. I almost don't want our number to come up because I have so much learning to do. I need to learn all this stuff. I am writing as fast as I can. And, incidentally, by the way, it says here that the RMV is happy to let us know that they accept our credit and debit cards. That is such a relief. They're so helpful. Just look at all those numbers they're calling. They're so efficient. What a nice place this is to be.

It takes about twenty minutes for the Kool-Aid to wear off, and then I am suddenly alarmed. I look around me at the rest of the room, at all the glazed faces looking up at the screens or staring out of their bodies into space, and I understand that I have just woken up in a holding tank for human life. As long as the distractions hold out, we'll be okay. But the distractions aren't holding out. I feel a little rush of adrenaline and start pacing the back of the room. Nick laughs behind his eyebrows at me. I try to laugh too, but I'm not doing such a great job at it when the electronic voice calls our number, and we take care of our obligations as new citizens of the state of Massachusetts.

On the way home I tell Nick that I have absolutely no conclusions whatsoever regarding any of this. I don't want to talk about it. I will make no attempt to communicate it to my mother-in-law. But then we open our front door and Bernie lets me take the sleeping baby off her chest, but only so she can go back to snacking on many small helpings of my homemade coffee cake. And I feel sure that this, somehow, is reality.

Whatever that was back there, going on in that waiting room—mediated by the television screens—was something else.

The next day Nick is back at the office and Bernie and I have the whole day together. I ramble on and on about the no Internet life. I'm cooking so much. I'm reading so much. I'm going to church. I'm healing all this old stuff from my youth. I'm just beginning to understand this, but it's all related in some way to my alternative upbringing as a child—I'm reawakening this old and different way of looking at the world.

I glance over at Bernie and stop short. I've been letting loose for several minutes, pouring out all my feelings. But Bernie is leaning back on the couch with her eyes closed. She realizes I have stopped talking, and her eyes pop open. She apologizes. She says she doesn't know why she is so tired. She says she isn't good for much.

"Oh, please," I say, "I don't mind. It wasn't important anyway. You want another piece of coffee cake?"

But I'm lying. I do mind. I don't want her to be sick—or old. I want her to be the grown-up one and keep me off the hook forever.

Bernie stays with us for the rest of the week, but the whole time she isn't herself. I ask several more times if she'd like to see someone. Boston has its faults, but none of them is a shortage of doctors. But she says no. She'll see her usual doctor as soon as she gets back. She's in no hurry.

I sit back and force my hands to be still. I wonder how Bernie got to be so good at waiting. I am not that good at waiting. Is this what a lifetime has taught her? Or is it what digital technology has taught me: that there is nothing in the world that I should wait for?

That night the rain begins. It rains all night. The rain and wind lash against our windows, like relentless toddlers. I relapse. I stay up all night staring at a screen, picking through and sorting my massive collection of digital photos that I keep on my computer. It is as close to the experience of the Internet as I can get using only my own data. I watch my family go by in bits and pieces, and then I spot my own reflection in some videos I made of myself, and I stop to take a nice long look. If I had Internet access, I would have Googled myself and read all the results. Even the ones I wrote myself. Especially the ones I wrote myself.

It is nearly dawn when I turn away from my laptop. I should just go to bed, but instead I drag out the heavy photo albums from the drawer. I am passing back, back, back through time, through my wedding pictures, the pictures of wild theater kids in college, the more intermittent photos of high school. There's a whole series of me and Jacob with our dog. Finally, in the very back of the cupboard, I find what I think I have been looking for the entire time: the photo album my mother made for me when she made a photo album for every child shortly after her divorce. I watched her then, sitting on the floor, weepy and nostalgic, sifting through the stack of glossy publicity photos from the height of her fame. Most of the publicity shots feature the middle sister as a baby on Mom's hip, and round them are the older boys and girls with wild hair. There is one of my father too, looking handsome like a cowboy, putting a bottle in a calf's mouth.

At the peak of her career, my mother gave it up to be with her children. Not knowing everything that was going to happen next, it was her only-partly-intentional suicide move. At that point she was a published author, a national speaker. She was paying on the 386-acre ranch and at times the sole source of her family's income. She was invited to do more television. She had this country-girl shtick, and the TV producers thought she was funny. They flew her down to Los Angeles to do the *Mike Douglas* show. The pay was $250 a minute, a fancy room, and a limousine. Show business. The catch was, she wasn't allowed to bring her kids, not even her baby. She came home from that trip and hung it up. She refused to do it anymore.

I wasn't born yet. The baby they wouldn't let her bring to Los Angeles was Jacob. I used to think it was so random and cruel, that she devoted her whole heart to her work when it brought in only pennies and suffering, but when she had the chance to be a star, she couldn't pull it off. All my life it seemed irrational and absurd. It seemed like failure. It seemed upside down. But now I wonder if when she held her tiny baby, she felt as if she had been running too hard and working too fast every single day of her life.

And if so, my mother and I are more alike than I ever dared to know.

It rains for three days. It makes me wonder if the sky is ever going to run out of water. It makes me think about eternity, and survival, and consider that if my shelter were any less predictably guaranteed, I would be gathering my loved ones around me and asking if anybody remembered where we kept those plans for the really, really big boat.

But on the fourth day, the sun comes out again. The kids and I burst out of the house like popcorn. We all go to my tree, where we see that the twigs have fringe, like halos, or little crowns—the majesty of spring. Something has happened. My tree has come awake. And it must have happened during the three days and ten inches of late-winter rain.

Is that where the spring is, Henry David Thoreau, my once-beloved philosopher? Is that where you found the essence of Walden? Would I have to be strong enough, or brave enough, or stupid enough to stand outside for three days in the Mortal Kombat rain?

But then it just happens. Like all the wonderful things you've waited your whole life for, it just happens. I forget completely that I'm supposed to be watching for the transformative, transcendent emergence of the spring because that day it is suddenly warm. It takes us all by surprise. Yesterday we were getting ready to build an ark, and today it's warm. But the sun makes me feel melancholy because it suddenly feels like San Diego and that makes me miss my friends. So much for being monastic and avoiding the messiness of being human.

The weather is beautiful for days. I play outside with the kids. I get a blister from my sandals. I resist the urge to pick up the camera. Instead I just sit there. I sit there and hold Stella's chest as unobtrusively as possible while she works on getting up and down the steps. I sit there and watch Milo. I watch him move from place to place and try to get the whole essence of him as I try to stitch the pieces back together.

The pastor at my church has asked me to participate, as a reader, in the special service for Good Friday. I immediately say "Yes," in the way that you say "Yes" when someone in a position of authority asks you to do something that seems important and you haven't done anything useful outside of your own home for several months. But I don't know what I'm getting into. I've never been to a Good Friday service, and I've never been a reader in a church service at all. Also, it doesn't seem like the right moment to mention to Pastor Jennifer that I have an irrational and debilitating fear of public speaking.

Pastor Jennifer has to drive to my house and put the readings in my mailbox because I can't receive e-mail, but she pretends that this is perfectly normal. I think pastors are often good at pretending that unique life choices are perfectly normal. I take the small sheaf of papers out of my mailbox and look them over. It's the first play script I've had in my hands since Stella was born. Immediately, the old muscles start to engage. I flip through the pages, assessing the drama, the language, the players, the staging, and the arc.

It's all shaped around the last seven sayings of Jesus before he died on the cross. Pastor Jennifer seems to be working with the subversion of power structures, which I think is a good choice. It will appeal to her highly educated and intellectually rebellious congregation. If I had to describe it, I might say Brechtian. Pastor Jennifer has planned to station me, a slight and newly baptized woman, up in the high pulpit of the historical cathedral. A male theology professor will take the mic on the floor. She herself will occupy the middle ground, the dais, and the three of us will alternate reading sections of Scripture and analysis and exhortation as Pastor Jennifer snuffs out the candles, one by one, and the overhead lights in the church are slowly dimmed.

I think it's quite wonderful. I wish I were directing it, or writing a paper on it. I'd be very good at that. But now I have to do the part that terrifies me, which is to actually show up.

On Friday afternoon I make a soup, and I'm sorry when all the vegetables are chopped, because the rhythmic action has kept my hands from shaking. I take the train into the city nearly an hour early and walk slowly all the way across the park. I am still early. I sit in the grand Tiffany sanctuary and listen to the choir rehearsal as waves of irrational fear ripple through my body.

When the service starts, I fall into a rhythm. During a hymn or a prayer, the fear subsides, and I can concentrate again. But when the hymn ends, the congregation reenters the normal time, and the fear returns. I fight through it, as I have done many times before. I accomplish what is asked of me, blindly following the directions on my page, until finally I am standing at the pulpit, my hands gripping the podium, and it is my turn to speak out the words of the crucified Messiah. The crowd is cruel, and he offers not cruelty in return, but the opposite. He says, "Father, forgive them, for they know not what they do."

These words come out of my mouth, and as they do, the world shifts. In my rational mind I am thinking something like "Huh. This fearlessness in the face of death is really a counter-example. Here I am afraid to speak some words right off a paper in front of maybe thirty people. I should perhaps give this some additional consideration."

But the rational mind is not in charge. Beneath it I am in some kind of flood. Some unnamed force is rising up in me, rushing through me, and lifting me against my will. My back straightens, my breath settles, and my hands rest on the podium like dead things. I think to myself, oddly . . . "Oh, Death, where is thy sting?"

I do not have language to explain what is happening to me. But later I will tell people that it was a miracle moment, a kind of healing, in which Jesus moved in on me and lifted me and swept away my fear. Some people will nod and understand. Others will consider it crazy talk. But many will ride the center, just as I do, unsure of what it was that really happened, but all the same humbled, challenged, and amazed.

There is a story. I don't know where this story comes from, but far away and maybe long ago, it is a story about a woman in a village. The village is taken by a warlord, whose reputation has preceded him. He is known for leaving no survivors. When he arrives, the village is already empty. Every soul has fled except for this one woman. The warlord is enraged by her cheek, her courage in the face of certain execution. He orders her brought before him and cries out, "Do you know who I am? I am the one who can take your life away with a single stroke of my sword." She answers him, "Do you know who I am? I am the one who can let you."

This is the kind of power I have borrowed for a moment from the crucified Christ. I felt it. Real and coursing in blood. Not theoretical at all. Though I might understand this power in theory and feel appreciative of it in conceptual form, I had never in my life up to this point felt its reality: the tremendous, earth-shattering power of forgiveness.

The service continues. I have more things to say, and so I say them. But the audience is gone. I am no longer conscious of our theatrical conceits. My performance, for perhaps the first time in my entire life, is not my primary concern. Instead, I hear the songs, walk the spiritual journey, feel the suffering. I lift my eyes to the stained glass all around me—the shapes and images of my spiritual heritage—just at the moment when they are nearly too dark to make out.

I am having a spiritual experience that I cannot analyze, cannot intellectualize. I am experiencing something in my body more real than my own bones, and I know as well as I have ever known anything that I will be forever obligated to this experience. From here on, I will never be able to undo my conversion.

When the sanctuary is completely dark, a bell rings. Pastor Jennifer says the ritual words, "Go now to your homes. Our Lord is dead." I walk at a brisk pace down the long aisle, out the tall doors, and into the half-dark of the city street. At which point I break into a run.

I feel a flash of guilt as I dash past a cluster of somber congregants whom I now know by name. But I have no ability to explain and no will to rein in my boundless, liberated energy. It is socially appropriate at this hour to be somber, but I have never in my life felt so free.

Five

My Mother's Money

My first memory is of the floor in a tiny kitchen. The lino-
leum was cracked. I was three years old. My father had
survived a serious illness, but the drug that saved his life had also
broken down the bone structure in his hips. Now he was in the
hospital, again, for one of several major surgeries. The money was all
gone, the 386 acres subdivided and sold off. It was 1982.

On that particular day, my mother happened to be in the hospital as well, getting an emergency hysterectomy. She didn't want
it, she wanted to have twelve children, but there was something
wrong. My oldest sister, Dolly, was taking care of all the little ones,
me included. I remember the smell of the soup cooking on the stove.
I remember my sister telling me not to touch it. I remember reaching up to grab it.

I remember being in the shower with my clothes on. I remember the sound of my own screaming. I remember the hospital, where
a nice doctor put pigskin all over my chest where my own skin had
been burned off. He gave me a little piece of the pigskin to play

with. I thought he was wonderful. They brought my mother in to see me, post op, in a wheelchair. She was wearing a thin robe over her hospital gown. I remember that she couldn't hold me. Whether it was her wounds or mine that prevented it, I'm not sure.

This is my first memory. But it was like that for my family for years. Crisis after crisis. The bad luck came in waves. We lived in a trailer. We lived in a car. We lived in a basement apartment that flooded every time it rained. My father left when I was five and became an elusive character in all our lives: a loner, a cowboy poet who offered endless fascination but no escape from the waves of hard luck crashing over us. The older kids started leaving too, one by one, until it was only me and Jacob left. My mother did try to work as best she could. She cleaned a church. She cleaned a rich lady's house. But her soul was the soul of a writer. She would always end up back at her typewriter, studying and teaching and preaching about a different way of life.

My adolescent years were the hardest. We rented rooms in a house that made you want to walk on the other side of the street. There were always gaunt and hollow-eyed characters hanging out on the porch. Jacob would have his friends drop him off a couple blocks away so no one could see where he lived. His room was downstairs. I shared a room with Mom on the second floor.

We had a door in that room that opened out onto thin air. There must have been a balcony in better days, but in our time that door opened out onto nothing, ten feet above a wild rose bush and a rusted Oldsmobile. We had another door that opened into the common area we shared with a revolving cast of the poor and disadvantaged. It didn't have a lock, and I don't know that I care to tell you which door was more dangerous. We had the room for $200 a month.

Our poverty was nothing to write home about, not for a single-parent family with a female head of household in the '90s. You could say it was typical. But it was a million miles away from the charismatic book author who went on TV and made everybody laugh. It was a million miles away from 386 acres of fertile land in Western mountains, with the orchards and the swimming hole and the swinging bridge.

Everybody has some kind of rise and fall. My mother had hers like a rock on fire. Her dream school, the School of Country Living, failed miserably as a business venture. Her personal relations became strained, her human capital all used up. And then in 1979, the same year I was born, America's mood turned into the dawn of the Reagan era, and the time of my mother's fame was past.

She did a new edition of her book. She was always doing a new edition of her book. It was updated, with new information and the most current resources. It was still a five-pound book, still big enough to hurt your thumb if you dropped it, still packed full of skills and information, a complete map of agrarian-centered life-style captured as it left the collective consciousness. But America didn't care. It might as well have been a paperweight. In the '90s, all we had for counterculture was Pearl Jam and striped tights. Nobody cared about growing their own food. Nobody cared about living off the land. And my mother's teenage children lived in a rooming house with junkies and the lost.

I rarely tell this story, in full, to anyone. Certainly no one at my Boston church has heard it, and it has never been displayed in any form on the Internet. But this is Holy Saturday, the Saturday of Easter weekend, the day of Jesus entombed. What is so transformative to me about this era of my embodied faith, so terrifyingly and reassuringly real about Jesus, crucified, is the way my suffering meets his. At the tomb, I am held and known in a universal language of loss and hurt. And if I am challenged to the power of forgiveness, to heal my hurts, I am challenged right from that deep core where even previously unspeakable suffering is known.

Easter Sunday dawns cold in New England. The east is light but not glimmering. The sky blue but not iridescent. The ground is soft, not grassy yet, but mud. We put our babies in their best clothes and all go together to the church, which is flooded with extra people, the once-a-year churchgoers like I was on Christmas Eve. There is a meal of hot-cross buns. A brass band plays. Everyone is wearing nice clothes.

I cast about for that palpable presence I felt at the Good Friday service, but it's gone. It seems to have vanished with the dawn. Everyone around me is proclaiming the good news, but I am not sure what good news we all are talking about. It feels performed. It feels affluent and safe. It feels like Easter bunnies and pretty dresses and tulip trees. It feels like not the same church I ran from Friday night.

Pastor Jennifer catches up to me. She says, "I didn't see you leave after the Friday night service. Were you okay?"

"Yeah, of course," I reassure her, even as I feel a shiver left over from what I experienced in that Good Friday service—that sheer vulnerability of the cross, that place at which there are no defenses left against the gospel, because it is so selfless and so pure. I can't and don't try to explain that Easter, for me, is by far the harder sell. Resurrection for me does not become real in a church full of well-fed pretty people wearing hats.

Some church members engage Nick in conversation. They've gotten to know me and are curious about Nick. I walk with Stella all around the sanctuary and look at the stained-glass windows. I want to chase all the people away, away from the tender, miraculous Jesus I met in the dark. I want back that other story of resurrection— as much as it frightened me—told in the way my hands stopped shaking, the way my fear was banished like light falling on a shadow. I don't know what hot-cross buns have to do with that.

We take the kids home to prepare to celebrate the same holiday in secular style. Nick has already helped Milo to dye eggs, a project that made them both smile and made my kitchen smell like hot vinegar. In the afternoon the kids nap and I spread the colored eggs around our front lawn for an Easter egg hunt.

The family that lives above us in the shabby red house is going somewhere. They come out their door on the side of the house, walk along the pebbled walk through the front yard and through their own separate gate in the chain-link fence. The toddler races through our yard, cackling like a wild thing. He picks up one of our just-hidden eggs and enthusiastically crushes it. One has to admire the young man's sense of purpose.

The grown-ups are already in the car, both the child's young mother and the grandmother who supports them all. Sent back to extract the toddler from our lawn is a boyfriend, who appears to be a rather shady character. He points to the crushed egg in the toddler's hands and says, "It was like that already."

I nod. That isn't true, but I offer no disagreement. I am familiar with this—the compulsive dishonesty of the addict, as clear a sign as his lurching sideways gait.

I busy myself with checking the mail as the broken Easter egg is redeposited on our lawn. The toddler runs, again, still cackling, but this time runs toward the car. When they are safely out of the yard, I wave and call out, "Happy Easter!" But they don't respond.

I've been so worked up, leading into and coming out of my participation in that Good Friday service, that I have for days completely forgotten about the mail. There is a whole stack of junk mail, coupons for local businesses, a letter from a California friend. There is a flat envelope from one of my sisters, which I open immediately. There is no note except a little "I [heart] you" scribbled on the inside flap in my sister's hand. Inside is a check for $3,200 made out to me. Five years after my mother's death, my sister is distributing the royalties from the most current edition of her book.

My mother always told us this would happen. She swore that it would happen. She had determination like a freight train, and she said the times would turn again. She said her people would remember her and would be grateful for all the work she did. Someday people would be so glad that she had compiled all this information that otherwise would have been lost.

She used to say to me, "Esther, when my ship comes in . . ." All I could do in those days was roll my eyes. But now the decades have turned, just as my mother said they would. Now climate change and GMO foods and depleted soil are issues for the newspapers. Now off-grid living and alternative lifestyles are topics for the mainstream. Now voices like my mother's are called "prophetic."

Today the organic food movement is rising. The slow-food movement is actually a thing. Everywhere you look there are local cooperative farms springing up to feed organic vegetables to yuppies. The appeal of food self-sufficiency and disaster preparedness is spreading well beyond the anarchists and the libertarians. This is the world we live in today. My mother's book is leaping off the shelves.

When the bank is open on Monday, I take my mother's check to the teller and deposit it into my checking account. I think better of it and move half the money into a savings account. Then I think better of that and move the rest of the money into a savings account. I don't know what I'm going to do with it. It feels like this money is carrying my mother's soul.

I'm already in the middle of a mind-over-money revolution. The check from my mother only sets the gears spinning that much faster. The groundwork for this revolution is four months of living without a debit card, which changes more than I ever dreamed it would. This is certainly not the kind of transformation I was looking for when I first laughingly dreamed up the adventure of a year without the Internet. But here I am.

I am changed because of the mental clarity of having so little digital distraction. But I also changed the practical negotiations. I have to use cash to put gas in the car, cash to put money on Metro cards to take the train, cash to buy used books at the thrift store on Tuesdays. If I want to buy a treat when I take the kids out for a walk, I have to have the cash already in hand. And to get the cash, I have to make a stop at the bank in daylight hours. I have to have a person hand me the money, and I have to tell them how much money I want. This is a level of accountability I had resisted with all my power, but now crave.

On top of all that, I'm having an unexpected triumphant experience with my taxes. Taxes, who knew? Until this year I had never done my taxes any way but on the computer. But without the Internet also means without that electronic friend/not-friend who asks a lot of prying questions and then counts up your refund like a scoreboard at a sports arena.

I considered hiring a so-called "expert" but felt that I couldn't justify the expense. I agonized for a day or two and considered cheating. But I am too stubborn to cheat. Once I finally sit down to climb my Mount Olympus taxes version, it takes me four hours and approximately nine square feet of dining room table. I emerge completely superhero triumphant.

DIY finances. It's blowing my mind. This is reclaimed territory, taken by sheer force of will, this precise knowledge of what money is coming in and how it's going out. It is territory I didn't even realize I had lost.

I prance into the kitchen with the finished forms and show them to Nick. "Look what I just did. I just did this!"

He sets down his cookie sheet and says, "Of course you did. That's you, baby. 'Nothing-Halfway' Esther."

I suppress the urge to walk him through every detail of the math, step-by-step, because it isn't the beautiful web of calculations that gives him authentic pleasure in this moment. He is proud of me because I did a thing that you're supposed to rely on an expert for, and I did it myself. And he's happy because I put in the effort to do this thing . . . for us.

Possibly because I want to hold on to the feeling of accomplishment, I become essentially obsessed with money. Performing arts was never the career for me. I should have been an accountant. I open the deep and overstuffed drawer that holds all our financial records, and by some extraordinary, inexplicable urge, I start reading. *Reading.* I am *reading* my bill drawer. Bill stubs. Pay stubs. Bank statements. Credit card statements. Promissory notes. As I soon discover, all this is high drama. Way more shocking than anything on TV. I swear to the great powers of credit and debt that I will never ever, ever again call economics boring. These are not documents that induce yawns. They are documents that induce panic attacks.

Thousands of dollars in debt? Stuff it in the file. Paying more interest than principal? Stuff it in the file. Your employer insists that you are going to grow old someday? Someday soon? Great Scott, man, stuff it in the file!

I don't know how I got this brave, but I look at every single document, every scrap. Hundreds of things are thrown away. I acknowledge that I have kept many of these papers only because I couldn't bear to read them. I tried to freeze them here, in my eternal financial adolescence, carbonite clad like Han Solo in Jabba's palace, or, better yet, like Snow White with the bite of the poison apple in her mouth. I shudder to think I could have died this way, financially asleep. There would be only a one-inch clear plastic tab to mark it, The Tomb of the Unknown Debtor.

I go back to my calculator and start doing different math. Not counting the money from my mother's book, which is a category of its own, we could be saving money at the rate of several hundred dollars a month. I mean, we *could*, if we didn't spend it all on things we didn't really want anyway. We could pay down our debt. We could get rid of it all in three years. It would take discipline and a certain kind of austerity. But wouldn't it be better to get free? Maybe after that, if we weren't slaves to all this debt, maybe my husband could spend more time at home. Maybe we could fix this thing we've broken.

I sit down at the dining room table, across from Nick, with the debt tally in my hand. I tell him what I've been thinking. I tell him I think it's time. Let's make a move. Let's change the way we do things.

He blinks. "You really think we could squash the student loans?"

"Yeah, I think so."

"How?"

"Just do what you already do. Scavenge. Bake. Cook from scratch. Fix things. Resist the urge to take your wife out on expensive dates."

That gets a smile, but he is still unsure. "It's just a matter of will. And sticking with it. I really think we can do it."

"All right." He shrugs. "I'm in." He is less sure about the money than about the way I am unequivocally treating us as a pair. He sees me treating us as a team of two, moving forward into a future that is together—after a decade of separate checking accounts—and sees it as a vote of confidence in us. I'm just excited that he trusts me.

I designate a notebook, where we write down every expense, no matter how small, from coffee to thrift store books to rent checks. (This one is not cornflower blue; it's black.) I'll tally all our spending in a spreadsheet at the end of every month, and this way we'll zero in on living rich instead of careless. We're more in control of our finances than we have ever been before in our entire lives.

Less Internet, more financial control. Who knew?

On the eighteenth of April I turn thirty-one years old. I receive one birthday card in the mail, which is thrilling, but it is made a million times more thrilling by the fact that it contains a gift card to Amazon.com. It was sent by someone who either doesn't know or doesn't remember that I'm not using the Internet this year. I think it's brilliant. I cackle into my hands like a banshee, "It's a gift card. Get it? To Amazon!" Nick closes his eyes and wrinkles up his forehead. Jacob says, "I hope it doesn't expire."

But I don't care if it does expire. I am not dreaming of online shopping. I am not dreaming of any kind of shopping. What I am dreaming of is social networking. It is my birthday, and social networks specialize in birthdays. I wonder how many birthday messages I have today. Surely it is a lot. Surely they are complimentary and admiring. Surely I have a host of adoring fans. "It's weird," I tell my longtime friend Emily, who has driven up from New York to make me a birthday dinner, "it's like a couple hundred people are throwing a party for your birthday at a club you can't get into."

Yet their club is not cooler than mine. Jacob comes along in time to enjoy Emily's cooking, and he hands me a CD on which he has recorded an original song composed just for me. I slide it into my laptop and immediately hear the sound of the mother board, the soothing electronic sound of a computer brain. When we were very small, Jacob used to taunt me by chanting, "Esther, fester, she's a sore." Now, as my laptop automatically opens the track in iTunes, my brother is accompanying himself on the ukulele as he sings:

> *You're not a fester,*
> *and you're certainly no sore.*
> *You're my awesome sister Esther*
> *who lives practically next door,*
> *and you've gone five months without the In-ter-net.*

"Almost five months," he clarifies, when the track ends. "I rounded up."

"Oh, shut up!" I retort. "I'm good for it."

Emily has given me a gift as well, besides the dinner and the visit and her sparkling conversation. It's an organic orchid planting kit complete with a little pouch of soil and packet of seeds. "You're going so crunchy. I thought it was appropriate," she says.

Nick nudges me. "Making things from scratch?"

It's hard to imagine how Facebook could give me more precious, or more challenging, things than this.

My little storm of money obsession has pulled energy from all my other pursuits. Books are left unfinished on the desk. We have eaten store bread and beans and rice for dinner. But I still keep up my three chapters a day in the Bible, and I keep going to church.

In the weeks following Easter, my church has lost her swell of once-a-year churchgoers and become her fragile, childlike self again. The performance quality that turned me off on Easter fades away altogether. And my strange miracle experience of forgiveness conquering fear begins to fade as well. I could almost say that I imagined it, except for the continued presence of Jesus—Jesus of the brokenhearted, Jesus of the suffering—that still challenges me to humility and amazement and . . . hope.

I still sit in the back, but I have revealed myself in too many ways. The sanctuary is no longer big enough to hide me. The liturgist seems to look right at me as she talks about consumption and justice, our call to serve the poor. This is my church at its best and also its most ridiculous. The service theme is on predatory lending, and though in reasonable terms we must admit that on this issue we are completely powerless, still, the sermon is unmistakably a call to action. We are David. And this—the poverty, the suffering caused by poverty—is our Goliath.

I wonder if God does things like this on purpose, shooting a message right into prepared ground, since I am already thinking of little else but money. I look around for a champion, but we are only thirty-odd sinners in spring coats, scattered like marbles through a damp though no less majestic Tiffany sanctuary. After the service, I fall out of the church with all the others into the wet, gray street and avoid the eyes of the homeless people as I walk to the train.

New England spring is messier than I want it to be, more fickle like my heart. I still keep looking for the page to turn, as it does in Milo's picture book, from white glossy winter to full, flowering spring. But we have only daffodils pushing up in pure mud, and the sun is cold. I sit on the porch, waiting for the mail and watching Milo ignore his toys in favor of the tiny pebbles that make up the upstairs neighbor's front walk.

The only personal item in the mail is my bank statement, which I open absentmindedly, still watching Milo. The junkie boyfriend has spent the night upstairs again. He comes down the pebbled walk now, stepping awkwardly around my son, and goes to the window of an idling car. He leans in, briefly, and just as quickly the car pulls away.

On the way back he realizes I have been sitting there, and he begins immediately to create an elaborate untruth, something about needing to purchase a new car. I nod and smile, thinking only that I want to avoid any possible conflict. The junkie is satisfied. He lurches up the walk and up his steps, with my son's blue eyes on him the entire way.

I return to my bank statement. It is short. In my cash-only life, I make all my withdrawals on a weekly schedule and always in person from the bank. But today there is something wrong. There are overdraft fees, related to the check I deposited from my mother's book royalties—an unusual check that didn't immediately clear. I have a fee for each time I moved my own money—my mother's money, that I couldn't decide what to do with—in transactions executed by a bank teller, in person, standing right in front of me.

I remember that interaction with the teller in the magenta coat. She noticed that April was my birthday month. Why didn't she tell me? That I was overdrawing my own account?

With fees and interest, the damage is $30. I want that money back. I load the kids into the car. I will speak out to the money giants, of which my bank undoubtedly is one.

I have on my Idaho-girl smile, which Boston people don't really understand is battle garb, when a customer service rep named Irene ushers me in and begins to nod impatiently as I rush through my prepared speech. She understands what happened, okay, but she doesn't see the problem.

I try again. "The teller didn't tell me that my account was being overdrawn. She was standing right in front of me, making these moves from one account to the other. She didn't tell me I was going overdrawn. Why didn't she tell me?"

"The teller doesn't have that information."

"What do you mean?"

"The teller can't see how much money is in your account."

"Why not?"

"The computer isn't set up that way."

"So it wasn't a mistake?"

She shakes her head. "No."

I find this chilling. Everything about my interaction with this slight woman, probably just about my age, is chilling. It is chilling that human beings are performing financial transactions and don't know the toll being exacted because of the way the computer is set up. And it's absolutely bone freezing that nobody at the bank thinks that this matters. I can't face the enemy because the enemy is nowhere to be found. He's been replaced by a computer.

Irene is glancing toward the clock, creeping its way toward five o'clock.

I stand up. "I'd like to just get my money out of here. Can I just have my money, please?" I can't close the checking account because I use it, and there is at least one check not cleared, but I will make what move I can. I will walk out the door with at least the contents of the savings account—$3,200 of inheritance from my mother's book.

"Are you driving?" Irene asks.

"Yes."

"Good," she says. "Be careful."

Oh, good grief, I want to say to her, is there anybody out there who has a more effective way of stealing my money than you? You work for the money giants themselves, and you want me to be scared of the five-minute drive down East Squantum? Suddenly I feel as if I'm dealing with the Mafia. I am no longer under the protection of The Bank. I am endangering my children by prancing around North Quincy with a pocket full of $100 bills.

But I don't say this out loud, to fall on stone ears. There is a river between us now, as wide as two tales of the creation of the world. I tell Irene that I'm grateful, really. I appreciate her efforts. Then I pick up Stella, I pick up Milo, I pick up his free lollipop, and I pick up $3,200 in cash. I say thank you and good-bye to the security guard, who has to use a key to let me out.

It is a clear and sunny day. I drive straight home and carry my kids into the house, where I take thirty-two hundred-dollar bills out of my pocket and file them with my unused credit cards.

The next time I get a piece of mail from our bank I open it eagerly, entertaining for a moment the absurd notion that they have changed their minds, that they care about me after all, like all the billboards over the freeway say they do, and that they are writing to me now to apologize. But it is only business as usual: a set of preprinted checks that Nick could use to turn his credit line into cash, paying an exorbitant interest rate and a 4 percent fee.

I am crestfallen and know perfectly well how ridiculous I must seem. But Nick sees the poison too. "Look!" he says, putting on an announcer's voice, "you can spend this money! And give some of your money to me! And I'll walk away with it forever! And it's *good* for you!"

I smile gratefully and turn my nose back into my book. Nick rips the checks up into little pieces and makes extravagant animal shapes out of them. They are still there, breathing in the movement of air across the dining room table, when I wake up in the morning and turn on the light.

I spend most of the day reading the Bible. I am a little too much for the world, lately. Maybe a little too intense. But I am not too much for the Old Testament prophets. "The people of Israel and the people of Judah have been utterly unfaithful," says Jeremiah to a wicked world. "Utterly. . . ."*

My mother liked to use that word, *utterly*. I stomp through the kitchen and take my $3,200 out of the box that holds my unused credit cards. I pick up Emily's fancy organic orchid birthday gift, dump out the contents, and hide my mother's money under the bag of dirt.

---

* Jeremiah 5:11.

Six

A Shade in the Garden

In May the people begin to spill out of their houses. There are older folks with gardening gloves, hanging bunting on their porches. There are flower bulbs coming up, teenagers hanging out. I watch the neighborhood the way I used to watch my Facebook feed.

There's a Hitchcock movie called *Rear Window* that my mother liked. There is a certain handsome fellow with a broken leg and a spy scope—and an extremely attractive girlfriend—and he spends all his time watching the neighbors. He gets to solve a mystery and catch a murderer. I doubt for me there will be any drama like that, but what else is there to watch? I do still read. But it seems out of touch to be always indoors and always in a book now that it is May.

Nick wants to be outside too. His work schedule is slowing down as the university looks forward to summer break. He sands and fixes up the wooden wagon he made the summer that Stella was born. He buys an old tricycle on Craigslist and fixes that up too for Milo. In the evenings he bakes or sits at his grandmother's antique sewing machine and mends the kids' clothes. I curl up in whatever corner chair is nearest him, picking up my book and then setting it down again to tell him things.

It feels more purposeful than ever before, this funny way we have of scavenging and thrifting and wanting to do things with our hands. We already make our own bread and cook meals from raw ingredients. I wonder how far we are from making a piece of clothing from scratch. It's funny. Our leanings toward handmade and salvaged used to seem like a kind of style choice. It was the way we located ourselves in relation to other people also locating themselves. But in a world free of avatars and profile pictures, sitting at the sewing machine isn't a style choice. It is reality.

Is this the answer, I wonder aloud, to that deep dissatisfaction that has so many times driven each of us to speed and distraction and other hamster wheels? Is this all we needed all along? To be more engaged in the underlying processes that fuel our lives?

Nick nods and looks far away, and I wonder what's going on under that skull of his, and whether it involves wearing overalls and chewing on a stalk of grass.

Soon enough I find out he was dreaming of free pallet wood. On his way home from work, he spotted a stack of abandoned pallets marked "Free." He now has dragged them home and stacked them against the side of the house. He is going to use them to make raised garden beds for growing vegetables. They will be my birthday gift.

He is pleased with his idea. I am alarmed. Although there is no gift I love better than reclaimed, repurposed trash, I think . . . garden boxes? Nick and I have talked now and then about gardening, extending our conversations about money and ethical lifestyle, and where our food comes from, and what it means to do things with our hands. But I entered all these conversations in theory, with a book in my hand. I was talking Thoreau, not gardening gloves. In real life, I don't garden. It's worse than cooking.

But Nick has already begun to strip the boards, humming slightly into his beard as he works. I would like all this change, and also I wouldn't. What I'd really like to do is get back on my social networking and waste a hundred hours a week and not feel any responsibility for any of it—not for my lifestyle, or my financial freedom, or the health of my soul.

This is such a wild, heavy thing. To say, "I will choose the way I live." It's audacious. But the biggest trouble with it is that it works. And, with our pace dialed down and electronic distractions all but eliminated, it is hard to ignore that I have been making these choices all along, whether or not I chose to be aware of them.

Change is possible. I would like to say otherwise. I would like to go back to bed. I would like it to be winter again. But April has come to an end, and the sunshine is relentless, as is the invitation of the warming, fertile earth.

Milo and I go to the window to watch Nick take the pallets apart. He takes off every single board and meticulously pulls out all the nails, then cuts off and sands every rough or broken edge. I love to watch my husband work. He always loosens up with the work of his hands. He becomes a little easier, a little taller, more vibrant. I fell in love with him this way, sitting on the workbench, my feet dangling, in the backstage of the student theater at the University of Idaho where we met, watching him put together sets for plays like *The Incident at Vichy* and *Fiddler on the Roof*.

Later, when I was a hot-shot director, I would hire my husband to design the scenery on all my shows. He was two-thirds of everything I had to offer. He was a gifted designer, but most of the magic was that he could build anything out of anything, and if I asked him to, he would. For an anime-inspired fantasy, he built a flying dragon. For a romantic comedy, he made it rain onstage. Doing a Greek tragedy in a very tiny theater with no crew, he rigged a tent so it would lift up off the floor into classically draped completion when an actor pulled on a single rope. He built airplanes and towers and a rolling bathtub. He hung sheer curtains so they would hide the scene shift but reveal the action. Sometimes he stayed up all night, crafting these imaginary worlds. He made them beautiful and perfect the way a craftsman does. And he made them for me.

One of the last shows that Nick and I did together, at the same theater where I would walk out of a rehearsal and destroy my own career, was a farce that needed a whole bunch of doors. Each door was different. There were the balcony doors, outside door, closet door. Half the game of putting up a farce is working out and timing all these doors. At the end of the act, coming into intermission, the bathroom door was supposed to spin around in place. The drama of the moment depended on it. Our first baby was due three days after opening night, and at that point Nick and I were both taking more work than we could handle. The design process was strained. Nick said, "You can make the moment work some other way, can't you?"

I said, "No, I can't. It *says*, right there, spinning door. The villain is supposed to be just standing there."

He said, "Let me put it this way. You can have a spinning door. Or I can make our baby a crib."

As I remember it, I didn't think the question deserved an answer. I got my spinning door.

Milo is tugging at my pant leg. He wants to be out on the driveway with Daddy. He wants to "help." "Okay, okay." I lift him onto my hip and slip through the chain-link gate. We both watch as Nick measures and cuts and stacks the boards. Then he lets Milo walk alongside as he carries them out onto the front lawn and lays them out in shapes, right on top of the wild, overbearing weeds.

It is the Saturday of Mother's Day weekend when Nick finishes the pallet-wood project. He comes to get me. On either side of the porch are two big, deep garden boxes. "Are they okay?" he asks, as gruffly as you might expect. He really, really wants me to love them. I can feel it. And I'm trying to.

"Yes. They're okay. They're perfect." Which they are. Everything about the garden boxes is perfect, except for me. I am "Nothing-Halfway" Esther, and the switch, when it comes to gardening, is off. I try to suggest that maybe Nick should be the one to plant the garden, but he says, flatly, "No, baby. This is you." He has already purchased a cubic yard of rotted compost, which fills the back of the truck, and he is wielding his shovel nimbly.

That night, after everyone else goes to bed, I take my mother's book down from the high shelf—five pounds and nine hundred pages of expertise on food production and food self-sufficiency. I open it to the chapter that is an introduction to gardening, which is right before the chapter about food preservation, and right after the chapter that tells the story of how my big brother Dan, as a baby, had croup. There is a garden plan. There are directions of some kind. But I can't see the words clearly enough to read them. My mother is too alive in there. It's like a séance. I set the book down. It stays open on my desk all night long.

Very, very early in the morning, I sit down at my desk and listen to the birds. The starlings are picking again in that ugly yard next door. To my surprise I discover that I am writing a letter.

Dear Mom. You're dead. I miss you. Could you please come back and teach me how to garden? Love, Esther. P.S. I don't think I'm kidding. Please?

When Nick wakes up, hours later, to make me French toast with strawberries for Mother's Day breakfast, I have my eyes closed and my head down on the open book. My ear is pressed down, as if I think the book is going to speak to me.

Unfortunately for me, it doesn't. May is in full bloom, and I still don't know the planting dates for Boston. Afternoons, I walk around the neighborhood with Stella in the wagon and Milo ahead of me on the red tricycle. I stare at other people's gardens. The flowers are in. Some hobbyist gardeners have cold frames. The contrasts across the neighborhood are dizzying. Here, behind a picket fence, beyond neatly mown grass, is a tilled and tidy patch in the backyard. Right next to it are three dilapidated houses with paths dug all around their front yards, haphazard trellises, and fence-lining dirt beds.

The most impressive backyard garden, maybe four or five houses down from us, belongs to Stu, who sits out in his wheelchair on warm days and yells at the passing cars to slow down. After I walked by and he identified me—he knows which house is mine but doesn't know my name—he wheels down the pitted sidewalk to our fence line for a chat. Milo is playing in his sandbox, ringed with weeds. Stella is sitting on the porch steps, working over an apple with her eight small teeth. I make a point of greeting him. I don't want my kids to be afraid of wheelchairs.

"Fifty-five years I've lived in that house," he tells me. "Fifty-five years."

"Wow!" I'm trying to be comfortable conversing with a stranger, though this isn't my comfort zone. "You must have seen a lot of changes to the neighborhood. What's different?"

"Well, the Chinese moved in," he said. "That's the big thing."

I don't like where this is going.

"This one used to be Italians," he says, gesturing to the house next door. "But they sold it. Now they're all Chinese. I know the lady owns this place too." He nods at me knowingly, as if certain that I will share his perspective. "Isn't she something?" His voice drops. "One of them *swamp rats.*"

I turn and pick up Stella to get her back to the porch. This is too much. I can't be in this conversation anymore. I have Chinese-Americans living on both sides of me. The city of Quincy is nearly half Chinese. There are Chinese markets and Chinese community centers. I can't imagine what it would be like to walk through this neighborhood feeling distaste for more than half of its inhabitants. I can't imagine it and I don't want to. I am picking up Stella to take her back to the stairs.

But Stella won't let me. She doesn't want to go back to the stairs. She just came from the stairs on her just barely walking toddler legs. She is already a headstrong personality, the kind of baby that makes you pick your battles, and she likes Stu. She wriggles down out of my hands. She wants to touch the wheels on the wheelchair. Stu looks at her and she looks back, and it's like they recognize each other from somewhere, long ago.

"Well, hello there," he says. "I guess you're a firecracker."

Stella shows him her eight teeth. The two of them have a standing date for the rest of May. I come out onto the porch, after her nap, to read my books in the sunshine and wait for the mail, and Stu wheels down the length of three houses, making an arc around the place where the tree roots have cracked the sidewalk in front of the home of our Chinese-American neighbors, whom I have never met.

I **continue** to try to engage with community. I am getting ready to take a vegetarian lasagna to a new mother in my church when a woman comes up to the fence. I am standing in my yard, obsessively going over my map and my directions since the drive is at least half an hour and I will have no electronic assistance. The woman says something. Her English isn't very clear. She points to her car. I am baffled. Then, Oh! She wants help with an infant car seat. I leave the lasagna on the porch and my children in the fenced yard and hurry over.

But right away I remember that I'm not very good with mechanical things. I am trying to get the darn seatbelt to lock down when I hear Stella scream. She had climbed up the bottom porch step and tossed herself back down. I run back into my yard. She's fine, just mad. Peaceful Milo is watching from his sandbox. I carry them both quickly to my car and strap them in.

The stranger looks upset but gestures to me that it is okay for me to go. She understands. I hesitate. Stella is perfectly safe now. She even has a snack in hand. Milo does too. But the stranger, I'm sure, can figure out the car seat better than I can anyway. I wish her a nice day and go back to studying my directions.

It isn't until I am backing out of my driveway that I spot the baby. My next-door neighbor, a young Chinese-American woman I rarely see and have never once spoken to—and why is that, anyway?—is standing on her porch holding a newborn. It is swaddled, tiny, wearing a cap. Two weeks, maybe. Three weeks, tops. The mother is wearing the look that all new mothers wear—a little wobbly, a little shocked. Fragile.

I am figuring this out. I am driving away with a lasagna to another white family in another neighborhood, when there is a newborn right next door. I am figuring this out. I turn around. I am coming back. But by the time I get back, it's too late. My neighbor and her friend with the car have either figured out the car seat or they haven't. They are in the car and driving away.

I stand in my dining room, behind long, heavy curtains, and watch my neighborhood. I watch the family on the other side of us play mah jongg on Saturday nights. I watch a middle-aged couple arguing in Chinese beside the car, young couples making out on the street corner in the dark, old women smoking cigarettes on porches in the morning. I'm amazed at how alone we all are, each in our separate existence, living as close to one another as we do. We are experts at not seeing one another.

Right above us is a middle-aged woman with an extremely energetic toddler grandson. In the nine months that we have shared exterior walls, we have conversed about three things: parking, snow shoveling, and the cost of hot water. We pay utilities separately, in each half of the house, and she wanted to make sure our clothes washer was hooked up to our own water line so she wouldn't have to pay for it.

We are sharing the air in the basement, each sorting children's clothes out of our separate washers into our separate dryers, when she tells me that her grandson is turning two this weekend. They're having a birthday party on the driveway, and can we move our cars?

"Of course. But what a funny chance! Our little Stella is having a birthday this weekend too. Is it the same day?" Their birthdays, it turns out, are only two days apart, and the parties will be held at exactly the same time. Stella is turning one. My neighbor's grandchild is turning two. That's about all I have for conversation, and I am relieved that she is gathering up her clothes, when suddenly she leans in and says, a little fiercely, "My daughter's got problems."

"Oh?"

"She had a baby real young, and the baby died. Ever since then she's got problems."

"Oh. I'm sorry to hear that."

"She went away, for help, but then she came back, and now it's bad again."

I nod. I think of the man with the sideways lurching gait who lied to me about a broken Easter egg. She's warning me. That's something like relationship. She says, "The party starts at three o'clock. We'll have hotdogs. You can come."

Looking through the windows on the day of the party, I see that it isn't exactly my crowd. I pause to put on my trained Idaho-girl neighbor smile before I step through my back door, which is right into the middle of the party. I have to watch that I don't step on anyone's fingers as I walk down the steps of the back porch and set my plate of homemade cupcakes and a small wrapped gift on the table right beneath my bathroom window.

I wish the little one a happy birthday. I ask if everybody's having a nice time. The young mother stares at me with something between blankness and hostility. She is tattooed and wears a silver dragon around her neck on a black cord. She takes the gifts in her hands but doesn't look at them.

I smile the biggest Idaho-girl smile I've ever smiled and rush back inside, where I casually close the drapes and move into my own daughter's birthday party. We eat lasagna and green salad around the family dinner table under streamers and balloons. We light a candle on the little round from-scratch chocolate cake made just for Stella, and then we sing "Happy Birthday" to our baby. After we sing it, Milo says, "Sing it again," which we do, and he's right. It is just as lovely the second time.

Our dinner cleanup is well under way when I hear the song begin again outside, and suddenly I long for more, more, more of the magic of a child and a birthday cake. I pull back the drapes and sneak my nose up to the glass. But the child is below me, with his back against the wall. I can see only what he sees, which is a battalion of cameras and camera phones, all raised up in front of people's faces.

My daughter's birthday unleashes yet another point of change for me, in what is feeling like an avalanche of change. I have made the decision to become vegan—to remove from my diet all animal products—as my breast-fed baby has reached age one and released me from certain nutritional responsibilities. The trouble here is that I am both cooking and reading. One or the other might have been harmless enough, but both together necessitates the change. Cooking my own meals, I have the ability to change what I eat to suit my values. And from reading the details of industrial meat farming, I have all the reasons to do exactly that.

In this part, I am not reliving my childhood. Like most rural people in the cold of zones 4 and 5, when we lived on the land, we lived on the animals. We drank the milk. We ate the meat. Long ago, before his illnesses, my father hunted elk and deer. Even years after that, years after he divorced my mother and made a life with another woman, he kept a half acre at the edge of town, and summers he kept a steer for meat in the back pasture.

Visiting our dad from our city life for one week at Christmas and two weeks in the summer, Jacob and I once tried to name the steer. I would have gone for something like Clover, and Jacob for something like Twisted Udder. But Dad growled at us, as he was prone to do to children, and said, "That's not a cow, it's a steer. And its name is Dinner."

Jacob had the vegetarian thing early, possibly from precisely that moment, but I went ahead and ate some Dinner. I visited again, later, and that time, I ate some Dinner again. Much later, when I was in college in Idaho, fighting the gap between my survival and my independence, my father would drive up to my place in his pickup truck and fill my freezer full of Dinner. I felt a kinship with those animals. My father fed the animals, and the animals fed his daughter. Though I found my father as elusive as ever, even more so when standing right in front of me, those animals did their very best to make us a family.

The cows we get from the grocery store are a parody of that kind of mutual care. With some part of my being, I have always known this, ever since I was a little girl and I watched my mother fight this fight about right relationship with Nature and the responsibility we ought to take when we feed ourselves. My mother believed in an exchange relationship with the animals. It was not theory; it was love. It was a deep and messy love, the way a person loves a dog.

I saw it up close, and I rejected it. I rejected the smelly pens and the muck boots and going out in all weather and having to shovel a path to the barn. I rejected it right out of hand, and I followed my peers like the Pied Piper into the meat aisle in the grocery store. But my mother's perspective seeped into my insides, into my bones. In my body, I have always known that at every point in an industrial meat animal's life, value is extracted from the exchange relationship to benefit the corporate bottom line. The sacredness is sold for money, leaving only the profane. The personal cost is something only God can see.

For birthdays when I was very little, my mother would rent the smallest possible TV and VCR, and every single kid would get to pick a movie. We would watch them all in a row all night long, like gorging on ice cream sundaes, and then fall asleep in front of the TV in a heap. When we lived in town and didn't have a car, my older brothers got the TV to our apartment and back on a bicycle.

The big kids would get *Star Wars* and *Back to the Future*; the little ones got those old Disney movies, like *101 Dalmations*. But my mother liked Hitchcock. *Vertigo. The Birds.* Mother's movie would be last or near the end, and I would catch little bits of it through dream-heavy eyes. A hysterical woman stepping out of a tower. A bird attack.

My mother's tastes would always turn that way. To her, the truth was always like that, tinged with sinister and likely to sneak up on our complacency. She warned in urgent tones that it was better to be prepared. In case of Y2K. In case of nuclear war. In case of an EMP—electromagnetic pulse. The drought, the fire, the flood, the earthquake. The second coming. These were not private feelings. She preached what she believed.

After the ninth edition of her book came out, she went out on the road again full-time. She shook hands and gave hugs, ate and slept wherever her people would keep her, and did interviews on radio or local TV. For months at a time I traveled with her like this, sleeping in the car. First a rainbow gathering and then a gun show . . . a night with the hippies and then a breakfast with the hard-right libertarians. My mother's people were all the people on the edges. All the edges, in every direction.

I was fifteen years old when we stopped speaking to each other, my mom and I. I was fifteen and a freshman in college. My acceleration in school was half my own and half my mother's doing. As representatives of counterculture, all of her children felt a certain pressure to prove the advantages of our way of life. But my heart was particularly bent toward speed. I loved nothing better than knowledge, unless it was competition, and my mother, the natural teacher, trained me in both.

I had no trouble gaining entry into various high-quality liberal arts colleges. I chose Smith College because it was a good fit for my young feminism, and I convinced my mother, on her cross-country travels, to drop me off there, in central Massachusetts, with all my belongings literally in one taped-together cardboard box. I had so little idea of what it meant to be an adult out in the world.

I did well enough in all my classes. Some upperclassmen exhibited jealousy when I excelled in a sophomore-level English class. I didn't dare tell them that my mother had taught me *Paradise Lost* when I was nine. It wasn't academics that challenged me. The snow in New England was fourteen inches deep, and all I had was a pair of beat-up tennis shoes. There were bills to be paid to the school that I didn't understand at age fifteen and with a parent who so fiercely claimed the simple life. I tried to get in touch with my mother, but she was still out on the road (these were the days before cell phones). I couldn't find her, and I knew that if I could have found her, she didn't have the money anyway.

Just before Christmas, by a clerical error, I got an extra check from my work-study job. It was a mistake, and I knew it was a mistake, but I cashed it anyway, quickly, before anyone could ask for me to give it back. And I used it to buy a one-way plane ticket back to Idaho. I called my cowboy poet father and asked if I could come and live with him. He was the only relative I could think of with a singular location, a phone number, and a home with walls. I sat in a lawyer's office while the lawyer drew up papers saying my mother no longer had legal custody of me. I mailed the papers to my mother's PO box, and the mail forwarding tracked her down. She signed.

For years, my mother and I didn't look each other in the eye. The space between us was like a lightning storm. She was deadly hurt that I had gone to my father instead of to her. I was just sad— sad from the inside to the outside and through every bone—that the mother I loved was a person who could not give me an easier time at life.

I stayed with my father for six months, the bridge until I was sixteen and old enough to hold a decent job. Then, from the summer I turned sixteen, I lived on my own, working night shift as an aide at a nursing home and nearly living at the university Theater Department. I had found my people in the theater. These were the misfits, the social outcasts, the bohemians. They became my new identity, my new sense of self. I had insomnia and bulimia and more than my share of cynicism, but I made out that it was all on purpose, all a style choice for a drama queen. And I pretended, for years, that my blood family was a bad dream that never really happened.

Still, all that time, even those years that I was living inde-
pendently and growing up free, my mother used to leave things on
my doorstep. I would come home from my classes and my rehearsals
and from work to find these things she had left for me. Leading
up to Y2K, she was trying to outfit me for disaster. A high-quality
sleeping bag. A Geiger counter. A case of freeze-dried MREs so I
wouldn't starve. A solar-powered flashlight. A wad of twenty-dollar
bills tucked under a bulk order of seeds.

That same year she went on a talk show with Art Bell in the
middle of the night. My big brother Dan heard the show by accident. He described this to me, what it felt like to turn on the radio
in the middle of the night and hear his mother's voice, warning and
advising, speaking to the nation about preparing for the potential
apocalypse to come.

She came to her children like that sometimes. Like a shade
in the night, like a veiled woman stepping out of a tower, like a
bird attack.

Most of my mother's seven children left the agrarian life in favor
of urban pursuits and secular values. But my oldest sister, Dolly, stuck
to the small town, rural way. She's come to visit us for Memorial
Day weekend, in part because her oldest daughter, Beth, is in this
part of the world and wants to show her mom around.

Dolly is, like our mother, a born teacher. She is someone who
can't stop teaching. She brings children's books for Milo and Stella
that she bought from a library sale, and when she sits down to read
them to my children, her voice is strong and lilting and sweet.
The children are enthralled. So am I. I think she ought to be on
the radio.

But as excited as I am, the visit promptly makes me very tired.
Dolly is not an introvert, like her isolationist hermit of a baby sister.

She is not, as far as I can tell, even the slightest bit afraid of people. Every day we go for a walk because we both like to go for walks. But there the similarity ends. When I go for a walk, I like to think about things, and then not think about things, and then think about things some more. My sister likes to talk to people.

On the boardwalk along the waterfront, she makes a point of starting a conversation with every single person we meet. She does this on purpose; it makes her happy when people engage with her. But it also makes her happy when they point to their headphones and glare and act like she is crazy. She enjoys the comparison between her value system and theirs. When people ask her how she likes Boston, she says, cheerfully, with her great big Idaho-girl smile, "It's a nice place to visit, but I wouldn't want to live here!"

When we turn away from the beach and into quieter residential streets, she starts naming the plants. We cross the parkway, and she stops in front of that same low bush that made me excited for the spring because I knew it would flower. She says, "Do you know what this is called? I don't know what this is called."

"No." I shake my head. "I have no idea."

"Hmm," she sings to herself, "that's too bad. It's pretty." We get home, and she starts to bustle around the kitchen. She knows hundreds of recipes. She writes out a few of her favorites for me in loopy cursive. There is a chicken curry dish. There is a yogurt and cucumber salad. My son loves cucumbers. He eats all the cucumber for the salad, so Dolly has to cut another one. But she doesn't mind. She looks at the two garden boxes Nick built and the small and random collection of not-yet-planted plants sitting on the porch and says, "But why aren't you doing cucumbers?"

"Oh, I don't know." I look at my shoes. "We just haven't planned it all out yet."

Dolly insists. We drive to a parking lot, where she spotted a seasonal plant sale. She buys a flat of four cucumber plants and shows them to Milo, saying in that gorgeous voice of hers, "I know a little boy who likes cucumbers." Milo beams and sticks out his little chest.

I fully doubt that these little green starts will ever produce a single cucumber. Not in my hands. I am just not a good gardener. Black thumb. Gray thumb. I am certain I will kill them. Out loud I say, "I don't know where to put them."

Back in our yard, Dolly turns her discerning eye onto my raised beds. "Mmm," she says, leaning over. "I would just tuck them into the corners. Like this." She gestures with her hands, loosely, how the vines will trail out of the boxes, across the grass.

I set the flat of four cucumbers up on the porch.

I tell Dolly I'd like her to see Mount Auburn Cemetery. This is New England's oldest garden cemetery. I do want to show Dolly the place, which is one of the most beautiful places in greater Boston, the sort of place where you can feel the cycles and patterns of the seasons all contained in something deep and true and enduring. But in truth, I absolutely must go to the cemetery today because if I have another conversation with one of my neighbors, I will die. I must take my gregarious sister someplace where there is nobody for her to talk to.

We spread our blanket on the first hill, not far from the grave of R. Buckminster Fuller. I am feeding fruit and cheese to my children and starting to relax when Dolly says, in that lilting, lovely voice that ought to be on the radio, "Milo! Come and see what I found!" She lifts up my chunky two-year-old. On top of one of the monuments is a robin's nest with three blue eggs.

I turn suddenly and glimpse something dark at the edge of my vision. Dolly is telling Milo all about the world, about birds, and eggs, and children. She is trying to read the dates on every single monument, treating my quiet sanctuary like a history lesson, and my son like he is the most important thing around. And this is the moment when I see her just at the edge of my vision, disappearing around a corner with her red ponytail swinging. I see my mother, as vivacious as the spring, and the lilacs, and the mud-splattered animals she loved.

My mother died when I was twenty-five years old. It was October, not spring, but warm in California. We had made our peace, as best we could, when I was in my early twenties, after maybe five years of hardly speaking to each other. She had visited me and Nick several times as she made her looping way back and forth across the country, giving talks to small groups on "The Modern Homesteading Movement" and "Self-Sufficiency and Preparedness." I was still horribly embarrassed by her, as she appeared in my urban rock star life. I didn't know how to fit her alfalfa-ready, farmer-girl persona into the life I had built around the stardust of the stage.

When I got the call, I was running the deck for the out-of-town tryout of a Broadway musical starring Chita Rivera. It was a good gig, lots of money, and something like prestige. The work itself was pretty menial, but I was rubbing shoulders and watching Chita Rivera dance.

The call came in just after the half hour, the magic time in theater when everyone puts away their own lives to get down to the business of creating our own reality. Shortly after this, an assistant stage manager will go around the dressing rooms to collect the valuables. It is a technicality in which we lock up wedding rings and wallets for actors so their things are safe while they're on the stage. But it is also a part of the ritual of the theater, a part of the launching sequence, the countdown to the opening of the curtain.

I didn't have my personal cell phone on me. I never carried my own life with me after the half hour. My brother Jacob called my husband. My husband called a stagehand named Christian, and Christian called me over the headset to meet him out by the back door. I took his phone in my hands, heard the words "flat-lined twice," and then I went down to the dressing rooms to collect the valuables.

It was a sudden and surprising death. Low blood pressure and an illness resulting in septicemia. No disease. No period of weakness. One day she was on the road, this time in Texas, selling her books and giving her speeches. And the next day, without warning, she was sick unto the point of death. Most of her children had complicated relationships with her, or at least complicated relationships with the counterculture in which she raised us, but not so complicated that we didn't gather around her as we could. After the show that night, Nick and I got in the car and we drove and drove and drove all night from California to Texas. But it was too late for me. My mother was already gone.

In the cemetery, Dolly is holding Stella's hands while she toddles around in her sandals. Dolly is teaching Stella how to walk. She can't stop teaching. She can't help it. She can't help what she does, which is name everything there is, like in the garden of Eden, like our mother did, teaching us the names of things. When our family drove across the country, rootless and unbound, we stopped at every interesting thing. My mother showed us meteorites. She showed us geysers. She showed us lands on which Native American blood was shed. She showed us shiny, large-winged bugs and canyons and capitol buildings. She showed us Shakespeare and Coleridge. And she showed us the riches of the spring: even to a robin's nest, with three blue eggs.

My sister isn't terribly impressed with my garden cemetery. Perhaps she doesn't know the exile's longing for nature. She, unlike so many of us, has never gone so far as to let that door fall shut behind her. To her, three blue robin's eggs are just an ordinary gift of spring. But she sits with me, patiently, as I keep my vigil into the birth of a New England summer among the monuments of stuffy Easterners and the dead.

After big hugs and good-byes, the children and I and Dolly pile into the car to drive to the train. Dolly is going to New York, and in a few days I will follow her to our other brother's house, where we'll spend a few days having a part-family reunion. But before I go, I have a job I need to do. It is almost June, and the cucumbers are still in their flat on the porch.

In the late morning, Stella naps and Milo plays with his trucks. Nick looks at me expectantly and says, "Where do we start?"

Immediately, as if I were a stage manager again and had cued the whole effect, it starts to rain. It is pouring down rain, the bucket-dumping kind of rain. I back up against the front of the porch and do okay, but Nick runs up the steps and gets completely soaked. He's all muddy. We shake with laughter. The day is wild. It's uncivilized.

We keep going anyway. What's a little rain? It isn't cold. We start by digging out flower beds along the fence and up against the front of the house. We are determined to tame this godforsaken lawn. Mostly we are digging up weeds. The roots seem to go on forever. We don't realize that the rain has stopped until a neighbor walks by with his small children and sees that we're planting a garden and says, "Oh, great!" We wave at him, the weeds in our gloved hands like tattered flags.

There is already dirt in the boxes. I set out the plants on the dirt. There is basil, peppers, tomatoes, brassicas, strawberries, cucumbers, and rows for seeds. Finally, I kneel by a corner of the raised bed with one of the cucumber plants, still in its plastic shell, and I raise the ghost of my mother. My mother in her straw hat, with her sleeves rolled up. She has gotten my letter after all and come to teach what she has to teach. Together we fall into the old familiar rhythm of planting. Dig the little holes. Move the hose. Drop each seedling. Tenderly pat the ground around each plant. Her hands, and my hands, together, in this dirt.

The next day my whole body aches. But May is new, new, new—new washed, new born.

PART THREE

the Sun

Seven

A Bitter Pill

I wouldn't mind if time would stop on me right here. There are sweet things and beautiful things that live only in the spring: the lush and green of the snow melt, the embrace of memory. I wouldn't mind if I could stay forever in this moment with my mother in the garden, in the opening and the softening and the tender growth of May.

But that is not the way things work. The calendar page turns, and spring dries out into the heat of summer. I don't know how I have made myself—on my soul journey—pattern with the seasons in this way. It isn't a choice. But I spend so much time looking at the sky that my soul grows into step with it. As much as I have come into step with the softening rain and the tender half-dark wild spring, I will also enter into the brighter light of summer. And I'm afraid I don't look as good under full sunlight.

The trouble begins with a challenging phone call with another sister. Sara is a mom, like me. We have kids the same age, and we find great solidarity and pleasure in our chats about potty training and babies who don't sleep through the night. But besides being kind and gentle and hilarious, my sister is also a fierce thinker, an uncompromising intellect. And it is this quality that catches a snag on the smooth exterior of my Year Without Internet.

I'm chatting with Sara on the phone about these letters I write to the Internet. At the end of each month so far, I have written an essay and sent it to my friend in California to post on my blog. Each one has been a sort of a wrap-up of key moments and lessons learned. There was the one about dropping politics, the one about embracing the ordinary moments of motherhood, one about managing my personal finances. The reason the letters have come up in the conversation is that I don't know if last month's lesson on reconciling with my mother's ghost is going to fit well in a blog post.

My sister isn't impressed with the question. "Why don't you just stop, Esther?" she asks with maybe a little more edge than she intended.

I don't have an answer. My closest-in-age sister, Sara is six years older than I am. We are similar in most every way, both built for observation, knowledge, concern for the hardships of the world, and love of beauty. But my sister could take or leave the Internet. I once thought this was because she has great strength of character, or because she doesn't struggle with self-obsession the way I do. But I have come to think it is simply a matter of birth date. My sister was born on the other side of the line.

I have tracked a line, these last six months. (I am looking forward to the research that will prove my anecdotal evidence; I assume my brother will tell me about it when it comes.) Whenever I tell people for the first time about my project, their responses fall into one of two categories. On one side of the line there are those who use the word "interesting," who wonder what things I have discovered. They use words like "implications" and ask, "Why?" These people are all older than I am.

On the other side of the line are the people who say, "How?" They are not using words like "implications" because they are looking at me intensely, trying to understand what exactly I mean. "How do you talk to people?" "Where do you keep your stuff?" "How is it possible to live this way?" These are the people who are younger than I am.

I was born in 1979, in the gap ahead of what we call the Net Generation. Right around my birth date, or just after it, is the rift we call the "digital divide." On one side, life is played out in pixels instantly and totally available, sped up and pressurized by the free content boom. But there are still people walking around, even right beside me, who operate in the other reality, where life is not pixels. Instead it is . . . what? Simpler? Quieter? I still don't know. I can't change what I am made of.

My sister Sara is profoundly kind and resolutely supportive. Always, no matter what I do, she is supportive. So why today am I catching this note of disdain in her voice? But I already know because I know my own disdain for this posture when I see it in others. I see it when people complain about things just enough so they don't really have to change them. It's a survival skill for all the post-boom generations. We all do it. It's like Criticism Lite. It's the best we can do.

How do I really feel about the Internet? Do I really think it's making me feel trapped and stupid and self-obsessed? Or did I just want to take a break from it so that when I came back I would be really super extra popular? I may have talked about spiritual growth and awakening and transformation, but my end goal was always a blog that gets ten thousand hits a day. My end goal was always validation.

Sara is offering me a kind but fierce challenge: "Why do you have to write these end-of-month letters? If you're going to go without the Internet, why don't you actually go without the Internet?"

I groan again, and this time not so much for effect. *I don't know.*

I don't know. I don't know. But by the time I hang up the phone, I have decided. Okay, yes, I will go off even this. Yes, I will stop sending these crusts of bread to my emaciated skeleton of a cyberself. I start writing a Dear John letter to the Internet. "I really mean it this time. No joke. This is the end. I am done with you. I have got to move on with my life."

If there is a difference between the experience of being off the Internet and telling people about it, and the experience of being off the Internet and not telling people about it, it's not a difference of degree. This is like going in the opposite direction on the same road. I prove the difference to myself by indulging one more time. I write one more letter to the Internet, which I title "The Red Pill," after the movie *The Matrix*, the red pill being the one Keanu Reeves takes to be ejected from the computer-aided fantasy into the reality of his post-apocalyptic world.

At first it is a list, an admittedly impressive list of *ten amazing things* that have happened to me in six months off the Internet. In pieces/parts, it is an impressive transformation:

1. I'm cooking. Real food. Using real ingredients.
2. I'm gardening.
3. I have read and completed forty-six paper books.
4. I am going to church.
5. I have read almost the entire Bible.
6. I am vegan.
7. I have more sex.
8. My husband and I have written and are following a debt-end plan.
9. I have letter correspondence with half a dozen friends, including my husband's grandmother.

10. It is a regular part of my daily routine that I look closely at a tree and watch the dawn break over the waters of Dorchester Bay.

There is a momentary rush of satisfaction. I am, after all, No Internet Lady of the World Awesome. But I know already, and better than ever before, that the rush I feel is temporary. My ten things are mostly an expression of the will I already had to mess around in my life and change things about myself and fill little notebooks. What I am doing is not wrong. I don't think there is anything wrong with me because I have this will to accomplish and to be the best and truest that I can be. But this is not really the part that matters.

There is real change occurring too. And the change that matters is not the change I mark on myself but the change that is being done on me, like a surgery patient having God's hand stretched right into the cut places in my heart. I know better than to think this work is anywhere near done. And I know, both because my sister said it and because I knew it anyway, that the next stretch is a test of my integrity.

I do my best to include this perspective in my "The Red Pill" letter. I try to explain the difference. Did I really want to be changed by this? Did I really want to bare myself to the sky and witness the world beyond the shield of my screens? Or was I only playing with my own reflection? This difference matters.

After I address my letter to Amy and drop it in the mailbox, I sit down on the porch to watch the dusk. My garden is already under attack only a week after I put it in. I don't know what is doing it, but I come out in the morning and find stalks chewed through by some tiny teeth. By the time I noticed it, two of my four cucumber plants were chewed right through. I asked Stu's opinion when he came down in his wheelchair. He said it was probably the squirrels.

I told Nick, and he made little cages to put over our plants, but by that time the third cucumber plant was chewed through too. There is only one left. I'm not convinced it was the squirrels. I think it might have been my house cat, who is responsible for knocking over stacks of books. Either way, it's not an auspicious beginning to my gardening summer.

As I am sitting on my porch, the mother of the newborn next door walks down to the street. I know it's her, but I don't have any way to start a conversation. I don't know where to begin. Apologizing for not helping with the car seat seems not a good place to start. I don't think she even realized I was there that day, and I don't think she would want to have a conversation about my guilt.

As I am trying to think of something to say, she begins to put a yard sale sign up on a tree with tape. This doesn't go well, and we both, in our respective worlds, find it comical. She looks at me, points to the tree, and says, "Doesn't work." I nod with empathy. This is a true point of connection between us. I, too, have recently told a tree that it was broken. She moves away, and I go in to get my kids ready for bed.

The smiles we exchanged are genuine. That's something.

The sky finds it appropriate to hail on their yard sale on Saturday morning. It is June, but the sky out here is like that. Not to be trusted. Possibly slightly vindictive. I don't know. They move their belongings up onto the porch, and I don't think very many people come around to buy. I don't stay around to watch. Instead Nick and I drive up to New Hampshire, with a road atlas and a bag of homemade snacks and $20 in cash. We find a state park and run around with the kids and play and look at trees and get filthy dirty and then put the kids back in the car and come home.

This is a rehearsal. Nick and I are practicing leaving town. We have learned that this is what people do in Boston in the summer. They leave. The students leave. The professors leave. The weather being what it is, I guess, everybody who has the means to leave will leave.

We have chosen what seem to be the most manageable and affordable destinations for escape—state parks as we find them on the atlas. The next weekend we get in the car again, this time with two bags of food, two kids, two tents, one Uncle Jacob, and the same road atlas. We do not have reservations, driving directions, updated weather forecast, or any guarantees. The state park system works. It is well marked. We drive right up to fresh brown paint and irrigation and manicured lawns.

I can't wait to go exploring. This park is called Savoy Mountain, and I go looking for the mountain. But by evening I am prepared to call the Office of Truth in Advertising to report an inaccurately named state park. "Don't argue with me," I tell my brother and my husband, neither of whom has any intention of arguing with me. "I know what mountains are. There is nothing here that qualifies as a mountain."

The hills are rounded, my hair is poofy from the East Coast humidity, and the firewood is damp, none of which would be the case in the Western lands of my birth. But mostly I am enjoying my right to be snarky, which is my identity as a child of Western wilderness. As night approaches we sit by the fire, and I comment to Jacob on the sense of peace it brings me, this slow gathering of night.

Jacob nods. It's so different from a light switch, this gradual change. You can't even tell exactly when the darkness falls. Maybe, if you're lucky, you forget to ask. This, I tell Jacob, is exactly what I'm talking about. This is the whole reason for the no Internet experiment, this mysterious gathering in of night.

When it gets really dark, we begin to eat. Because what else is there to do? We eat hotdogs, which are really a terrible excuse for food, and marshmallows, which I think are not even pretending to be food, and then finally the slow-cooking baked potatoes and baked apples, which are spectacular enough to burn our mouths on. We walk a little way from the sleeping children in our tent and look up at the stars. And they are no less beautiful, no less meaningful, no less magical than they have been for lovers and philosophers for centuries. There it is, I tell Jacob, all the pattern, all the context, all the perspective that a person needs to regain sanity in an insane world.

Nick is the first to spot the fireflies. I immediately forgive the poofy hair and the damp firewood, because Massachusetts has Idaho cold on this one. *Fireflies.* These are foreign creatures to me, and I find them absolutely amazing. Nick catches one and puts it in my hand. On and off. On and off. On and off. The mystery in my cupped hand. The mystery in a jar. I could bring these fireflies home with me, and then I could get a piece of this whenever I wanted. Or, I suppose, I laugh at myself, I could just get a light switch. I open my hands, and the firefly buzzes back into the wet, tall grass. I don't think they live very long anyway. If I had the Internet right now, I would use it to look up the life span of a firefly.

For the next three weeks we go camping every weekend, searching the thick forested hills of Massachusetts for something unnamed. But the magic falters and, on the fourth weekend, fails. Nick has worked late, so we are rushed and end up at a state campground on a lake, which on a weekend night is more densely populated than our street back in Quincy. As night falls we realize in amazement that our neighbors are having a birthday party, complete with Jell-O shots and appropriately obnoxious audio stimulation. They play "Sloop John B" and I sing along, "This is the worst trip I've ever been on."

We return to town and I go to church instead. But the church is odd, deserted. Here too everyone goes on vacation in the summer. Even most of the programs, even the Sunday school, will not resume until the fall. My first friend, Stephanie, is gone for the entire summer. Our friends Ian and Sarah have moved on with their exciting young lives.

I take the train home again, alone, and entertain myself by counting the number of people in my train car who are on their screens and headphones. I live way out on the Red Line, past the split, so the train is never full. People are sprawled out or bundled up. Sitting. Today there are nineteen people in this train car and eleven of them are using screens. A blonde woman gets on at South Station and she's crying. She is trying to read her book, but really she's crying. Nobody is looking at her. I am not sitting near her, and even if I were, I don't have any idea what I would say. Maybe "I see you."

I wonder how many cars there are on each train, how many trains there are in each city, how many cities. In every train car, are there eleven people on screens and one person crying? In every train car, is there one person going for a year without the Internet?

On the last day of June, the neighbors with the baby are moving out. They are packing and moving and seem to have many hours of work ahead of them as night falls. I go over and ask if I can help them with the work. But they are not at all happy to see me. They don't seem very happy in general. They send me away, saying they have help coming later.

I go to bed, restless and uneasy in the humidity, and wake up to the sounds of a screaming match. It is just before midnight. A white man in a pickup truck is shouting and revving his engine. He uses racist words. One of the young Chinese women is shouting back at him. It's hot. I put on my flip-flops and go out on the porch. The pickup truck is gone, but the young woman is still yelling. A young man catches her attention and jerks his head at me. Then they all turn my way, this slipknot of strangers with their boxes and furniture scattered across the lawn and lit up by the headlights of a parked car.

I shake my head. "I just came out to see if you were okay."

"That mother—." She's crying. So am I.

"I know," I say. "I heard. I'm sorry."

I'm already vulnerable and half cracked open by neighbors and train cars and sky when Emily comes up for another visit and finishes the job. She's noncommittal about her plans for her summer vacation from her job at the Metropolitan Opera, and I can smell like a hound when someone isn't telling me something. As we walk together with the little ones in the wagon to go play at the beach, I lay the pressure on her until she confesses. Yes, she is about to go on an international vacation with a once-very-tight group of our old friends, a gathering of glamorous theater types that includes the old friend of ours who slept with my husband. She didn't tell me this before because . . . well . . . obviously. I am not just sort of not invited. I'm completely not invited. Too much bad blood, too many things that happened. Emily is almost in tears from carrying all the tension.

"Oh, Emily," I say, "I know it isn't your fault." But I am deflated, shaken. I feel the loss and betrayal all over again. I feel the sorrow that even being off the Internet couldn't protect me from this grief. It doesn't matter if I am close to people or far away from them. Either way, they keep reminding me of things that hurt.

While the kids play in the sand with their little plastic shovels, Emily and I stand there together, on the beach, two Western girls looking out at the tepid and passionless Atlantic, and we talk about how lonely we so often feel. We talk about how weird and crazy it is that this loneliness could happen in the heart of our most vibrant cities—Boston and New York—that anybody could feel so abandoned and so alone. And yet we do. And we're not the only ones. So many people speak of this and feel this in our strange time. It is the era of hyper-connected isolation.

We all pack into the car to take Emily back to New York, then go up to Riverside Park. It is Fourth of July weekend and the Upper West Side is like an empty balloon, all free parking spaces and quiet tot lots, one of which we monopolize all afternoon in the perfect weather, to Milo's and Stella's delight. I walk over to Broadway and look down and see ghosts. All the actors who live in this town, the famous ones and the not-so-famous ones with whom I have had drinks and flirtations and hours and hours of rehearsal hall bonding, none of whom would probably recognize me now. I see all the people who told me I had potential and the ones who told me I didn't. They all live here. This is New York City, the center of the American theater world. And here I am with my children on a holiday weekend, eating Armenian food with a plastic fork. And watching dead things walking.

We give Emily our hugs good-bye and she gets on the train, headed downtown. We drive up to my brother's house, where Miriam tells me, again, probably not remembering that she told me before, that her neighbor is the president of an actors' union, and have I ever heard of it? I nod, yes. That is the union that I used to belong to and technically still do.

"What are the chances." "Right." "Well . . . that's New York for you."

Improbability notwithstanding, on this particular day the president of the Actors' Equity Association is standing in his backyard looking over the fence. My brother introduces us. I am charmed, as I should be, by that warm where-does-it-come-from actor's smile. I confess in my weakness that I have allowed my membership to lapse, making a noncommittal wave toward the children and, possibly, the sky. He suggests kindly that I should call to arrange an honorable discharge. Otherwise, he says, if I want to work again, I might have to pay a new membership fee.

I cannot imagine working in the theater again. What are the steps required to make Moses lead his people back into Egypt? But the nice man is right. I should do the paperwork. I say thank you and I wish him well on his current project, which is, of course, a Broadway musical. He probably knows Chita Rivera. Then I head back to the house and do my best to get down to the business of celebrating a national holiday.

Back in Boston, Jacob is aware of the sudden stream of sadness pouring out of us, and when we ask him to babysit so we can go to a movie, he immediately says yes. Nick has spotted a poster at a Yonkers bus stop for a movie he wants to see. All afternoon he has been trying to find out where that movie is playing and at what time. But of course he is at home, which means he has to do this without the Internet and without a cell phone. It isn't going well. Finally he comes into the room where I am reading and says, "I feel really isolated right now."

I close the book. "Do you want to go to the library to use the Internet?"

"I tried that. They're closed. They're on summer hours."

"How about the bakery down the street?"

"My computer isn't working."

"Do you want to borrow mine?"

"No."

"What do you want to do?"

"I don't know."

He walks away. I hear the opening and closing of kitchen cupboards. I get up and fold the laundry and change the diapers and then call Jacob to ask if he can babysit. Nick perks up immediately when he hears that I am willing to leave the house, and he decides that we will go downtown, to a Landmark movie theater that still has its schedule recorded on a phone line and is so prominently located that it basically actually is a landmark. We get Stella in bed and Milo ready for bed and try to help Jacob scrounge for dinner makings. Then my husband and I break the rules of our debt-end plan and go out to a movie.

Walking down the street without our kids is a sudden revelation. We hold hands and I do a little involuntary skip at the traffic light. Nick has my full attention, for a change. At least, until we get into the movie theater, and then he doesn't have my attention at all. My mouth is open and I'm staring. It's like culture shock.

Nick stands in front of a gray box and pushes buttons. I stand in the middle of the wide lobby and turn in circles and stare. I can't believe that all these people do this. Do we really show up en masse just to look away from each other and look away from the world and spend $8.25 on a cardboard box full of popcorn? I don't understand what's going on.

Nick hands me my ticket and, probably wanting to avoid another strange mood swing, doesn't hand me the receipt. We take the escalator up to the second floor, where the floor-to-ceiling window overlooks Boston Common. The sun is setting. The sky is all shades of red and magenta. I watch the colors shift while Nick buys snacks at the concession counter. People stream past me toward the junk food and the movies. Somebody is not looking where he is going and bumps into me. I apologize. The problem is mine. I am the one looking in the wrong direction. I am looking at the sky.

By the time we catch our outbound Red Line train going home, I think it's all completely hysterical. I'm making poses like the actors and repeating funny lines. I'm giddy with laughter. Nick and I can no longer understand the economics of movie-going. We can no longer understand why anybody would pay so much for so little.

This is odd, I suppose, for two people with college degrees in theater, but we can no longer understand the logic of placing your mind fully at the mercy of your entertainment. For two and a half hours, we were unable to read anything, or learn anything, or plant anything, or fix anything, or think for ourselves. All we could do was sit there and ride the movie and hope to God that it has more funny parts than boring parts, or that the actors are good enough to carry it even when their characters are thin. That isn't entertainment to us anymore. That's imprisonment. It is a mild and temporary imprisonment. Like an airplane or a dentist's chair.

So we say this to each other. We say it together, so at least each one of us is not alone. We are choosing to rank our cerebral independence more highly than our entertainment. We are choosing to value our creativity more highly than our purchasing power. We are changing, and the movement of this change is out and away from everybody else. It may be beautiful, it may be romantic, but it is also starkly, frighteningly lonely.

I tell Nick that it sometimes feels as if we are on a boat, just the two of us, and we are getting farther and farther away from the shore so that fewer and fewer people can understand us when we speak.

I try to speak across that water while giving Jacob a ride home. I want to explain to him why his assistance was so necessary today, how it happened that Nick and I are so fragile and so alone, how a visit from an old friend and the memories she awakened could drop us so instantly back into insecurity, and how destabilizing that is in a life where we have chosen to place our attention so fully and so exclusively on each other. I want to talk about family and community, how I can really see how this countercultural move could work if only we felt a little less alone. But nothing comes out right. As has been the case since the January snow, I find myself wrapped in layers and layers of white, fluffy sound-absorbing Me.

Jacob asks if I liked the movie.

I tell him I don't think I'll go to any more movies for a while.

He says, "You need to get out. It isn't healthy for you to stay in the house all the time."

"I know. I know. You're right."

"You need community. I know you hoped that the church would be a viable source of community for you, but unfortunately it doesn't seem to be working out that way. It may be time to start exploring other options."

"Jacob, I think my no Internet experiment might be running away with me a little bit."

"Ya think?"

His response is more callous than I expected. Less understanding. I want to pull over to the side of Longfellow Bridge and tell him he can walk the rest of the way home. I want to take him by the shoulders and shake him and tell him he should stop oversimplifying and stop talking about things he doesn't understand. But I don't do any of that. Instead I swallow my tongue and continue to obey traffic laws, at least as well as anybody else does in Cambridge. I try to explain a few more times and get tangled up in my own words. Then, in a last ditch effort to recover the easy intimacy of our brother-sister friendship, I ask him to tell me what's been going on in *his* life. He looks at me as if he isn't quite sure what I'm getting at.

Finally, when I have the car stopped and turned around in the little parking area next to his building, he turns to face me and says, "Are you okay?"

"Yes, I'm okay." We give each other a hug, and he gets out of the car, and I know that what I have said is absolutely true. I am okay. What is also true is that an era just ended. It has never before been true that I was going somewhere in life where my older brother couldn't lead. He has everything there, in that giant brain of his, rattling around with the authors and the types of rhetoric and the recent and most interesting studies in the field of human psychology. With all that knowledge and a decade of shared experience, during which he and I were children of the same unusual mother at the same unusual time, Jacob has always been the one who understands.

But he doesn't understand tonight. He doesn't understand that I can't give up on my church just because the people who are easiest to talk to are out of town for the summer. That isn't what I went there for. I can't give up on my experiment just because it isn't nearly as much fun when I'm not bragging about it all the time. I can't give up on the vulnerability of my spiritual search just because it walks me through dark places. I'm too fragile to explain. And even in his academic brilliance, my big brother isn't wise enough to know.

The next morning I conveniently forget that I'm at all concerned with the overconsumption of resources, and I stand in the shower until the hot water makes condensation on the ceiling. I remember how sometimes I thought of my Year Without Internet as a coming-of-age ritual—like my night on the mountaintop—and how I foolishly thought that it would be fun to do that much growing up. I said to people, "There's nothing like having a couple of kids to show you how much growing up you have to do." And that's true, so I set out for the mountain to get myself some growing up.

And now, look, good for me, look what I've gone and done. I've isolated myself from everything and everybody, even from the most precious relationship in my life besides my marriage. Is this what I came here for? Is this what I think passes for reality? It's like I fell out of everything and everybody, and now I wish I could get back in.

I stand in the shower with my hands in the falling water, and I know this is reality. I know it is reality that even your best friends can't think your thoughts. And it is reality that you don't always get to go on your vision quest with your big brother at your side. I also realize something else: How necessary and how vital this is for my husband, who is up here with me on this mountain—by his choice and by his vow—that I would stop putting my brother first, and in doing so let go of a thread that time had already cut.

I use every single drop of hot water in the tank to grieve the childhood dying. As kids, Jacob and I were partners in crime. He threw a rusty dart into my leg once, by accident, and helped me wrap a sheet around the hole like in a strange Renaissance painting so he wouldn't get in trouble for throwing rusty darts at his little sister and I wouldn't have to get a tetanus shot. Never before or since were two distinct motives so precisely aligned. It taught me the meaning of politics.

Later, when we were teenagers, Jacob would share his cool friends and his music with me, and I would worship him for it. He would introduce me to alternative low-budget theater and smoking cigarettes at bus stops—having no idea that I would become severely addicted to both—and we would listen to Camper Van Beethoven and stand back-to-back against a broken world.

In those days, I would have done anything to protect him. But then he moved away and so did I, and our mother was crisscrossing the country selling a dream, and our father was far away inside himself, and the world was hard on both of us. I wasn't there to see it when my brother grew up strong and became a man. I wasn't there to see it when he became a gifted teacher, and a writer, and a curio collector of rational ideas. And he wasn't there to see me when I gave up after one semester of liberal arts college to become a night-shift nurse's aide caring for the elderly and the dying. He wasn't there to see me when I gave birth to children and gave up my hard-won career in theater to save a marriage that would be a safe place for their utter dependency. He wasn't there to see me when I rejected my faith out of pure pain and lived a life without it and came trembling back to hope for what I'd lost.

Neither of us was there to see it happen as the brother-sister mythology of everything understood and everything shared gradually became, a little at a time, no longer true.

Eight

Hearts of Stone

There is a thunderstorm at three a.m. during the night I finish reading the Bible. Everyone else in my house sleeps through it. Even the cat is curled up contentedly at the end of the couch until I set down my Bible and pick him up, at which he mews reproachfully. I stand at the window and watch the lightning split the sky over our sleeping neighborhood, so full of humans having human troubles and feelings and human needs. I think of the promise recorded by Ezekiel: "I will remove from you your heart of stone and give you a heart of flesh."*

I'm not sure I wanted to find out that the problems of the digital age would be quite so transferable in spiritual terms. But this particular issue I face—being ruled by pride and not wanting to make myself vulnerable with others—is one that the Old Testament prophets anticipated with perfect clarity. They make the dressing of pixels around my heart look like nothing more than a fancy coat of rock.

Nick and I are both reaching, as best we can, to find a way out of our isolation. Our ways are different, but we're both trying to find a

---

* Ezekiel 36:26.

way to move together. I pray. I pray a lot. Prayer comes easily to me, though they are not very saintlike prayers, and I wouldn't want to show them on Instagram. I wheedle. I beg. I make deals. I say, "God, you get me out of this stone box and I promise whatever you ask me to do, I'll do it." I am young in my faith and not yet clear exactly how willing God is to make precisely this arrangement. Nor do I know enough to realize what I'm asking when a stone box can be broken only by force.

Nick and I have had so many shifts, so many changes, that we hardly know the people we are becoming. We honestly don't know whether it is normal for us to want to take a two-week summer vacation to visit his family back in Idaho. I don't know whose idea it was. I know that I wanted a do-over on the unsatisfying visit from Nick's mom back in the spring. And I know that everybody else in Boston leaves, so maybe we should too. I know that Nick is searching for wholeness in his own way. Though he is less extravagant with his soul searching, less drawn to spiritual transformation and public experiments, he is also, in his way, turning over rocks. Like me, he has completely left where he came from. Like me, he has lived into work and art and passions instead of living into his family history. Now, a father of two and carrying deep sadness, he feels a pull back to his roots.

I'm not very comfortable with Nick's family. Which isn't really their fault. My own family is so unique, so separated from the mainstream, I never know what to do with myself in regular houses, with TVs and sugar cereal and people wearing nice shirts and going to normal jobs. I don't ever know what to say, and have said the wrong thing more than once. But I am turning this way, toward my husband. I am trying to learn to trust and to follow. I agree to the trip as long as Nick promises that we'll do at least a couple days of camping in those Western mountains I love, like we used to do when we first met. Then I let Nick buy the plane tickets because I can't use the Internet.

The tickets are purchased, but the trip is still weeks away, when I tell God I'm offering a deal. I want to do and be something meaningful, and I still think church is a pathway toward that, as much as I resist and draw away and retreat into my heart of stone. I make a promise on a Saturday that I will go to church on Sunday, and I will accept the first invitation that anybody makes to me. As much as the attendees are scattered by the summer, there is always something going on. There will be a book club, maybe, or an adult-education class. Whatever it is, I will not say no. I will not make an excuse. I will show up and do this thing that is really hard for me—yet so clearly mandated in Scripture—which is engaging in community.

And maybe I will prove to Jacob that life still works, even on this side of the river.

Lately, Nick has been coming to church with me. He is still not motivated in any way to join, but he likes the kids to come and has made some interesting friends. He sits next to me in the long wooden pew as the announcements begin, and I strain my ears for my invitation.

The first announcement at church is for a gathering that will occur the very next day. It is a meeting of the group that facilitates our sister relationship with a community in Nicaragua. I don't know anything about the group, but I will go because I promised God I would. I know the people who are hosting. They live in Cambridge, very near to where Nick works. I call to let them know I'm coming, and she's very nice on the phone, although in that reserved New England kind of way. This is nothing to worry about, I reassure myself. I do live in New England.

I drive up to Cambridge with the kids in the car to meet Nick after work. He drives to the address, which is an unassuming gray house on a nice street, and watches indulgently as I stall in the passenger seat long enough to slam down three thermos lids full of coffee. I feel that a bit of nervousness is appropriate, seeing as how I am going to a gathering of people I don't really know, the subject of which I don't really understand, hoping that it will somehow save me from depression and isolation and irrelevance. Nick for some reason keeps smiling behind his beard. He says, "Go on, baby. You can do it."

The home is stunningly beautiful. There is tea and cheese. The meeting is jovially disorganized, in the way of church meetings. One of the members participates by speakerphone, like a disembodied voice floating up from the center of the heavy, dark coffee table. Picking my way through the chaos, a bit at a time, I gradually come to understand that what this group does is take trips to Nicaragua, that there is a trip in August, precisely adjacent to but not overlapping my Boise trip, and they are looking for one or two more people who might be able to go.

As they brainstorm names, I feel my eyebrows going up, and when they invite me directly, assuming—you can't really blame them for this—that it is an interest in Nicaragua that brought me to their meeting, someone clarifies that you don't need to speak Spanish and you don't need to be able to pay the cost of the trip. I realize that my mouth is open, and I close it.

I don't at this moment think about how I'm not a good traveler—I am *not* a good traveler—or that I convinced myself years ago that I am incapable of learning foreign languages. I don't think about the fact that I am so naturally introverted—lately more like borderline agoraphobic—or that our finances under the end-of-debt plan are so tight. None of these things occur to me. All I feel is a flood of relief. There is something for me to do. There is a place for me to be. And there is a God.

Because this—and I will sing all the praises in the world to this—is the God I believe in. This is the God who speaks through the mouths of pretty much anybody who cares and says, "Esther, did you say you were looking for something to do? Because I have an opening right over here . . . in Nicaragua."

All the way home on the train I rehearse how I'm going to tell Nick. Of course there is the baby, but she is ready to be weaned. She's over a year old. We can find a full-time babysitter to watch the kids. This is a city. It's for only nine days. What's nine days? They'll be okay. I come in the door and say, "Honey, I need to tell you something. Please don't be mad at me."

He laughs out loud. A big belly laugh.

"What?" I ask.

"I know," he says. "I already know. You're going to Nicaragua."

"But . . . how did you know? I didn't know!"

"I knew as soon as you went to that meeting on Nicaragua that you would want to go."

My husband looks at me, and although he doesn't laugh again, that rare feeling of the belly laugh is still clinging to his face. He says, "Esther, come on. I know you."

It is very like me and my husband to have this kind of knowledge gap, in which he silently fathers information at the very moment that I am blindly walking without it. The Nicaragua trip has been announced before. Either I didn't listen or was distracted by tiny children. Nick knew all along the purpose of the meeting and even the approximate dates of the trip.

So there it is. I'm going to Nicaragua. Nick has already thought about it, already decided not to hire a babysitter. His university job drops off to almost nothing in the summer, and he can get the time off work. In fact there are no obstacles to speak of. I repeat it over and over to myself. *I'm going to Nicaragua. I'm going to Nicaragua. I'm going to Nicaragua.* This is what you get, I guess, if you say "anything" somewhere where God can hear you.

Now that we have it all settled, I need the Internet more than I have ever needed the Internet because (I have to sort of whisper this part) *I don't actually know where Nicaragua is.* I've never been south of Tijuana. I don't have a single paper map in the house that shows land beyond the borders of the red, white, and blue. I do have a lot of books, but they're all from the Goodwill and not one of them is about geography. The best I can do is a section in *The People's History of the United States*, which is one of those books my genius brother recommended that I theoretically love but haven't actually read. As it turns out, in that book Nicaragua is treated as a part of the block of countries called "Central America."

At church and at after-church meetings, I receive packets and packets of information. There is more information than I ever dreamed I wanted, including maps of Nicaragua, although they show only the very closest neighboring countries, which is not enough to counteract my total failure of geography. The group of people who go to Nicaragua generally overlaps with a group of people concerned about immigration issues.

In the church basement, we all sit in a circle of folding chairs and talk about how many people there are who want to move to the United States and what a tiny fraction of them will be able to do so. We talk about the long wait times, the surprise rejections, the inevitability of people trying to move away from poverty toward economic opportunity. We talk about welcoming the stranger and following the call of Christ to die to the self and, most courageously, we place all this in the context of a broken and suffering world. This is my church at its best and its most ridiculous—like hope showing up to fight Goliath. I'm along for the ride.

Because I have been preparing for the Nicaragua trip, the previously scheduled trip to visit Nick's family in Boise sneaks up on me. We have swung hard, from having nothing at all to do and no one to talk to right up to being so busy I hardly have time to make the homemade bread.

The night before we leave for Boise, I write out a Dead Dog List, which is a list of things like Stella's blankie and the address book that are so important that if we forgot them we might as well be dead dogs. I do this because, although I temporarily forgot this when deciding whether to go to Nicaragua, I am a very bad traveler. I get frightened and flustered and flighty even when traveling short distances, and our flight out of Logan International Airport is at 7:00 a.m.

In the morning I am indeed flustered and flighty, and I run around locking windows and forgetting things and feeling stressed beyond words until we get in a taxi and I fixate on the GPS unit on the dashboard. I feel my breathing change, my shoulders relax. It is not the technology itself that calms me, but the way it captures my imagination. It is telling a story about our lives in motion. The little screen frames a movie plot in which the taxi is the protagonist, every corner an obstacle, and the destination is a tidy, achievable goal. I imagine that when we arrive at the airport, we might earn 100 points and a pleasant little dinging sound. We might even advance to the next level.

In Boise we stay at Nick's brother Luke's house, which is a suburban mansion compared to our four rooms in Quincy. I give their polished, pretty children Chinese junk food and falling-apart old books from my thrift store stock. There's no use in being self-conscious about it. It is what it is. As soon as I can possibly accomplish it without being rude, I escape into the backyard and look up at the giant blue sky. Little Sammy, my niece by marriage, takes me to the swing set, where she teaches me a song that goes, "I'm going high, high, high, in the beautiful sky, sky, sky."

That's it, really. It repeats, like a Top 40 song. She says I can go high, high, high in the beautiful sky, sky, sky too, but only if I swing as high as I can and lean my head back when I get to the top.

I give it my best shot, but my heels drag.

I throw the tennis ball for the dog. The sky is piercing. The oldest brother, Ben, is in gymnastics, and he asks me if I can do a bridge. I am immediately indignant. Of course I can do a bridge. I put my hands flat behind my ears and press my belly button up into the sky, rising up onto the balls of my feet. I am momentarily exuberant. Ben gives me a slight nod of appreciation. For several minutes after that, I can't stand up. I lie on my back, where I have basically fallen, and drink in the hugeness and the piercingness of the Idaho sky.

Unlike our visits to New York City, here we do not expect our hosts to accommodate my vegan diet. Nick wants to cook. I wonder if this happens to everyone—it happened to me and Nick—that when you feel a pull to meet the ghosts of your childhood, you find they want to meet you in the kitchen.

We drive downtown to the Co-op, a landmark of the granola crunchy side of Boise, the culture in which Nick first grew his hair long and bought a VW bus. I buy dry beans and spoon yellow turmeric powder into a plastic baggie. A thin man wearing an apron offers to let us taste a peach. I tell him we've come as visitors from Boston. He replies solemnly, "Idaho is always available, if you want to slow down."

I think I do.

Nick is driving his brother's car. Milo is back at their house blissfully playing with his cousins. Stella has fallen asleep. I'm not sure why it is taking us so long to get across town. It's a pretty small town.

As if in answer to my unspoken question, Nick says, "I'm kind of wandering. Is that okay?"

I shrug. "Why not?" I put my bare feet up on the dashboard. This is exactly what I used to hate about Boise. This is, in fact, essentially why we left—the way everything slows down, the way the space opens up and the sky dominates. The city loses against the land.

But this is the prize I won for everything I lost in these last six months. I learned how to unplug without disconnecting. I learned how to be fed like a plant, from underneath. I feel a thrill. The air is dry. My hair is lying down. We have come home.

Nick's mother, Bernie, is waiting for us, still wearing her oxygen. She reads to the kids, and the kids play with her, and we all pretend there's nothing wrong. We visit Nick's grandmother, my pen pal, Evelyn, with the long, sloping handwriting, who thinks she is going to die soon and wants to make sure I take a lot of her books. "I know you'll appreciate them," she says in a tone of confidentiality that is only slightly a backhanded remark toward the rest of her relatives. She has spread out some of her favorites on her bed. They are dusty and eclectic and fully worthy of a thrift store. Many of them are not worth ninety-nine cents. I take as many as I can carry.

In the evening we are invited to tag along with Nick's brother to a birthday party. Stella has just barely fallen asleep, and we let her sleep just a little bit longer by driving around. We have no destination, or intention, and are soon just as lost in the infinite grid of southern Idaho suburbs, zoned agricultural, as we would be in an East Coast rat's nest. I look out the window and all I see are expanses of green growing things.

We're going faster than the speed limit. The plant life swirls together, making psychedelic patterns. The car is moving too fast for me to focus. But at any speed, I'm sure I can't tell all these plants apart. Broad green leaves. Spiky green leaves. Green leaves. Green leaves. This is the food I eat, but I really have no idea what any of it looks like. I keep staring. Like a deposit of rock ore, somewhere beneath the layers of my life, I have a memory of driving through land like this with my dad in a pickup truck and hearing the sound of his voice. Sugar beets. Potatoes. Soybeans. Is this a ghost? Am I making this up?

I try again, focusing harder this time, but the memory is gone. Again I have no idea what plants I'm looking at. I force my will, trying to tune my memory to the landscape, trying to resurrect the connection, but it's hopeless. I am in the no-man's land of movement. I am moving past. Why do I always notice that I want to learn things just at the moment that learning is impossible?

Still focusing on the plants, I see emerging in the field two straw hats and three bare heads bobbing between the rows. Involuntarily I turn my whole body toward the glass.

Nick sees them too. "You wanna talk to someone about immigration issues?"

"No kidding." In the basement back in the church in Boston, it seemed so theoretical to talk about the workers who come from other places for these jobs. But there they are, right in front of me. So familiar, so constant, and yet invisible.

I feel like the land just let me in on some kind of secret. Where does our food come from? Who is it that can tell these plants apart? Who walks on this green earth to feed us? And is this why I want so much to understand the immigration issue? Is it because these are the people who plant and grow our food, and so they are my people, the people of my mother and her book about living off the land?

As we circle back through town, I look for signs of this second population. We are in a small town, an agricultural town, driving past a church with the sign out front in Spanish. Struggling to read the sign, I remember that when I get home, I will have only three days to practice my Spanish before I leave for Nicaragua.

When we arrive at our destination, at the house where there is a birthday party, the host comes out to meet us just as my father would have done. These are Idaho social graces. Grinning broadly, he introduces us to the animal pastured alongside the driveway, whose name is Burger.

The next morning I get up early and drive a borrowed car to downtown Boise. Boise is not only the home of Nick's family. It is also where my father lives. Our roots are farther north, up in the Idaho panhandle, near the college town where Nick and I met. But my father, a widower since the death of his second wife, has moved to the comfort of the capital city, where he lives in a turret apartment in a historic hotel, the walls lined with books. I have come to meet him early in the morning because there is something he and I both need to do, and we might as well do it together. It is to drive several hundred miles south to visit his mother—my grandmother—in her nursing home in northern Utah.

The conversation is constant for about a hundred miles. My father and I lift right out of the car, and right out of the rocky ground of our personal history and relationship. We are imaginative, thoughtful people. We are quicksilver thinkers. We speak well on esoteric things. My dad talks about political disappointments and quotes Yeats, "The best lack all conviction, while the worst are full of passionate intensity." This president, he says, is just as embroiled in the hogwash as anybody else, and the only thing left to do is to opt out.

He is about to make a move with his girlfriend into her dream home, a round straw-bale house in New Mexico. Dissatisfied with pretty much everything about the way the world works but particularly with a nefarious economic and political system, his plan is to just get out of Dodge. He says, "I may not be revolutionary anymore, but I will not be complicit." My dad is seventy years old.

We drive all day. It is early afternoon when we finally emerge from our air-conditioned car into the desert heat and then, just as quickly, into the air-conditioned oxygen of the nursing home. In Grandma's room, I see that the pictures of my kids I sent for Mother's Day are still in the envelope on the dresser. I pull them out and pass them from my hands to hers. "Did you see these, Grandma? These are Milo and Stella. These are my kids."

She takes the photos and looks at them carefully before making her pronouncement: "They're not mine."

She is bright and firm, with the characteristic lilt that makes me think of all the Mormon women I've ever known. They are so skilled at being very, very nice while also firmly and resolutely disagreeing. I take the pictures back and start pinning them up on her bulletin board, all the while feeling her bright and cheerful disapproval on my back.

"Are you visiting?" she asks.

Dad answers for me. "This is Esther, my daughter. She's here from Boston."

"Well," says my grandmother, freezing the bones in my chest with her good cheer, "welcome."

Right outside her window is that mountain I've been searching for in every one of those damp Massachusetts campgrounds. I tell her I appreciate the view.

"Well, I like it," she replies.

Dad tries a few more times to explain to her who I am, but

it's hopeless. She can't understand how I could be her grandchild because she no longer has grandchildren. She is shedding her memories from back to front, easing out from under the weight of her long life like a superhero bends the railroad tracks out from under the train. She is like a Bob Dylan song we have on vinyl: "I was so much older then. I'm younger than that now."

I think my life might be getting shorter too. It was a year ago that I last saw her, when we were on the move from California to Massachusetts. For a few hours on a Sunday morning, Milo alternately hid behind Daddy, crawled in and out of his sister's car seat, and suspiciously eyed the metal walker, while Baby Stella and I sat in silence and held my grandma's hand. On that day a year ago, she knew me as her own, although she could not tell me why. When I left, she said, "Please, come again," although she did not say, "I love you."

One year later, she recognizes only her son, and she is meeting as if for the first time the woman her son has brought from Boston. I don't blame her for my chilly reception. I'm not too sure about Boston either. I listen as my dad talks to his mother about family nearby and nursing assistants and hearing aids. She keeps her chin up. She holds on to her pride. But then the conversation goes dry. She is visibly tired. It is time to go.

I say, "Good-bye, Grandma. I love you."

She says, "It was nice to meet you."

On the way back, I am nearly sick with exhaustion. I almost go off the road. The conversation is thin, and I ask Dad to tell me the names of the crops, mostly just to help me stay awake. But we are no longer in the fertile valley, and this road is no breadbasket. There are only the badlands, where nothing grows except sagebrush. And then farther on, miles and miles and miles of feed corn, corn that will be mashed up, leaves and cobs and stems and all, and fed to the cattle I no longer eat.

The next day it is Nick's turn to drive. He has borrowed his brother's car along with a tent and some sleeping bags. We have more days than destinations. We wander through Nick's childhood hometown, a small town about an hour away. We haven't been out here in years. Nick is showing me around. The sledding hill . . . the grocery store where he had his first real job . . . the house he busted up as a delinquent teen . . . the park where he sometimes met his dad for the court-appointed every other weekend.

"I'm weirded out," he says.

I nod. This is what happens when you come back. Time fails. Geography wins. We're in the children's book by Margaret Wise Brown in which the little bunny keeps trying to run away, but his mother is always there, arms outstretched, embedded in the land-scape. This is what Idaho is doing to us. We are her children, and we are being claimed.

There's the high school . . . the wheat field across the street . . . the house on Kinsell Drive. I feel stuffy and hot. I roll down the windows and feed bananas to the kids and tell Nick I think it's time we were on our way. We turn north, and before long we are moving out of Nick's childhood country and into mine. By the time we hit the straightaway at the top of the grade, it is my turn to think with my snake tail and my monkey brain. I am staring at the trees and the rocks. They have something to say to me, and I want to get out of the car. My body knows this country, and it wants to get out of the car.

It takes hours to get up to Elk River, the little hunting town where we used to camp weekends in college, when we first met. The drive is charged. I can't relax. Even after we are parked and setting up our tent, I keep running like a dog in a meadow to look at this, see that. I don't want to miss anything.

It's harder than it should be to find our way around. The town of Elk River is still tiny, but the camping areas are more developed. There is a paved parking lot I don't remember being there. The trails are marked, and there's a fence around the waterfall where we kissed under the cold water as sweethearts years ago.

We dive into the cold pond like seals, come out again immediately, and eat white-bread sandwiches and potato chips we've assembled from the camp store in Elk River. The woods are a completely different experience with children. We used to fan out over the hills, ignoring trails, exploring fearlessly, fairly daring the large animals of the woods to find us. Now we stick to the path. Our children seem tiny against the tall trees. The big slippery rocks look like murder weapons. I don't let the children out of my sight.

We look for bird nests, although it is too late in the season for eggs. We catch a frog. We walk our legs tired and then settle around the fire pit to roast apples and potatoes, careful not to send sparks into the flammable brush around the majestic trees. I don't know what challenge or adventure I was looking for as a young adult when I left all this. I don't know what could possibly have been more of an adventure than the hills right around the town where I was born.

Still, I can't relax. Neither can Nick. As beautiful as the Elk River woods are, with the frogs and the jays and the dappled light filtering down through God's canopy, we both feel some tension, some unexplained urgency. In the morning we pack up our tent and eat more white-bread sandwiches and, promising to stop a lot on the way back, we load our kids back into the car.

For the sake of symmetry, if nothing else, I ask Nick to drive through the tiny town of Kendrick, where I lived before my parents were divorced. I am looking for the white house on Schoolhouse

Hill, where I remember learning to read, where Jacob and I slept on the floor in the living room with the walls and walls of books. I have a nostalgic memory of our last Christmas as a family, with apple cider and cinnamon sticks and all the Christmas songs. The steep walls of the canyon give me vertigo. At first I can't tell which house it was until I get my bearings and realize how much the lot has changed, as it should, in twenty-six years. I tell Nick not to stop the car after all. I am more stranger here than friend.

I am still looking out the windows as we cross out of Kendrick, traveling along the Potlatch River, past the swimming hole where I once got caught in the current and my big sister had to pull me out. There is a truck parked by the road. On the back of the truck, parallel to the road, are two 4x8 sheets of plywood tipped against each other, creating a vertical surface. Attached to that surface is a manikin lying horizontally, tied up in ropes with knots around its neck. In bottle caps above the figure, letters spell out "METH, NOT EVEN ONCE."

It is not an oddity. It's a campaign. All the way back to Boise there are homemade artworks like this one, in each tiny town, with the same slogan: "Meth, not even once." Skeletons hang from a tree. A poster-paint project over a soccer field: "Meth blocks goals." Around the outskirts of the city, glossy full-color billboards that remind me of the movie *Requiem for a Dream*, and nobody ever wants to be reminded of the movie *Requiem for a Dream*.

I am reminded of my upstairs neighbors back in Quincy, the young woman with the child that runs like a baby elephant over our heads at night. I feel my heart taken by this tragedy of addiction that sweeps through the ranks of the hopeless and the disenfranchised—in Boston, in the flophouses in Seattle where I lived as a teenager, and here. I am trying to connect the dots between all the lives I've lived and all the heart wounds I've tried to close over with stone. But I am moving too fast. I can only stare at the woods and the livestock and the fields, all moving past too rapidly for me to focus. There is no sense except the emotional sense, the poignancy of this collective cry, almost from the land itself, calling out the names of her beloved lost.

When we get back to Boise to return the borrowed car, Nick's brother isn't home. But we hear the news from our sister-in-law only minutes after we come in. Bernie has her diagnosis—lung cancer. The details come along in bits and pieces, but only one of them matters. This very likely will be the illness that kills her. It could be soon.

I don't retain anything more than this. For days I don't write anything down. We gather close to one another. We drink wine. We watch ridiculous television programs. There's one in which people go on a foam obstacle course and get knocked down by strange windmill-like arm thingies. I don't understand this. I don't understand why people put on silly suits and try to conquer silly obstacle courses. I don't understand who paid for the construction of that set, which cannot by any stretch be named either useful or attractive. And I certainly don't understand a fatal diagnosis. Who can believe that we are actually, someday, going to die?

I forget all about immigration and illegal drugs and the fact that I'm leaving for Nicaragua in just one week. Instead we go shopping and bring back food to cook for the dying and the vegan and the young. Nick bakes a crusty bread. We drink more wine. The world is bright and in color. Sharper, somehow. Tighter fitting. The air is bent. We feel close to Nick's family. We feel lucky we could be here. We feel glad we happened to make all this space, these days, having no idea that this is the thing that would come along to fill it.

But even a wrinkle in time is temporary. The gap closes. Our return trip to Boston looms, and divisions between our different families begin to reappear. We disagree over social issues, and I remember in a flash everything I was running from when I left Idaho. I remember the schism I have carried for so long between two groups of people I love. On one side the urban progressives and liberals who took me in when I felt like an orphan and gifted me my courage and my voice. And on the other the rural Christian conservatives of my heritage, women who gave me fresh cow's milk and Scripture, who despised feminism for undermining their value as full-time homemakers.

I go upstairs on the last night of this now-bizarre vacation in my brother-in-law's house, thinking about all the blood I spilled in this same war, all the time I spent sitting at a computer screen tossing out criticisms and opinions, widening with my own destructive force the split through my own soul, just because it is so much harder to face the true front in the war, the shared enemies of poverty, disenfranchisement, addiction, loss, and grief.

I pray again, begging God for a theology of peace. Christ in the space between, Christ as the bridge across this canyon, Christ as the third way . . . loosen the stone around my heart.

Nine

The Peace
of a Child

When we get dropped off at our front yard by a taxi, it doesn't look much like home. It looks like the second ugliest yard on the block. I can't imagine the little girl and her song about the sky in a yard like this, which is just a patch of unmown grass that nobody loves. I drop my bags in the yard and go straight to the one surviving cucumber plant to see if we have any cucumbers. We don't. There aren't even any flowers.

I go to the mailbox as Nick takes the kids inside. There are no personal letters, which is not surprising, since all my pen pals knew that I was out of town and two of them live in the city I was visiting. But there is a thin envelope from one of the credit cards that is dormant for the year of digital fast, which seems curious. I am sliding it open as I walk through the living room, and something odd catches my eye about the hope chest as I scan the single sheet in the envelope, which tells me that my credit card has been stopped because of a suspicion of fraudulent charges.

No. I shake my head. That's wrong. I didn't even have that

credit card with me while I was in Boise. Thinking that I will call right away to get this cleared up, I go to the half-hidden box where I keep those two credit cards.

But when I open the box, the credit cards are gone.

I rush to the hope chest, which I can see now is unlatched. Not open, but unlatched. Located so near the children's toys and so full of random preciousness that could be destroyed by children, we would never, ever have left it unlatched. I don't want to say this and make it true, but I have to tell Nick what's going on. I squeak, "I don't know where my computer is." He half lurches around the house and answers like a parrot, "I don't know where *my* computer is."

The truth of it hits all the way now, and I drop to my hands and knees and start shaking. It isn't even crying yet because the sound and the tears can't keep up with the crazy. It isn't the credit cards I'm crazy for. It is my computer. It is my photographs, and my letters, and my poetry, but most of all, it is all the record of this year without the Internet, which has been my anchor and sense of purpose when everything else seemed in flux.

My notes and photos were not backed up, and they were not printed out. It is gone. The Year Without Internet is gone. "That's what I've been doing," I say, shaking my hands as if I can shake the crazy off the ends of my fingertips. "That's what I've been doing, for months. That's the only thing I've been doing."

We think of the junkies upstairs, and we carry our children up the back stairs to knock at their door. Our neighbor opens the door with her grandson behind her knees, a bookend to our two children on our hips, and we ask if she knows anything about the white computer. We don't care about the silver one, I say. We don't care about the credit cards or the change bucket, or even the betrayal, or the crime; we don't have to tell anybody about this, but for the white computer, we could do something. We could offer some kind of a reward.

She shakes her head. She is blank and cold. We are hot and crazy. Milo keeps saying, "Are you okay? Mama, are you okay?"

We call the police, and now we are forcing our wills, trying to understand what we don't understand, trying to remember events we didn't witness. I forgot to lock the window in the bathroom. There are dried dirt footprints in the bathtub. There is a makeshift ladder made of junk piled up against the back of the house. Nick's computer bag is gone, with both of our memory sticks. His track ball. His foot-and-inches calculator. No drawers were left open, but on the insides of drawers, papers are ruffled and containers overturned. On the table is the note I left for Jacob, just exactly as I left it, and the stacks of mail, and dry crumbs on the plate that once held muffins, like Santa's plate on Christmas morning. The cat has recently been fed. Jacob must not have realized that it happened.

The crying has stopped, although the crazy has not, when I remember about the one-hundred-dollar bills. Ever since April, when I tried to meet Goliath at the bank, I have had my whole savings account lying around the house, in cash, first in that very same box where some desperate soul found my unused credit cards, then hidden in the not-yet planted DIY organic orchid that Emily gave me as a birthday gift. I go to the peat pot, which is adjacent to and almost touching the box that held my credit cards. And when I lift up the packet of seeds and the black plastic bag of potting soil, there are 32 one-hundred-dollar bills, curled up around one another, just exactly as I left them. And even through the shaking and the loss, I have to admit that this is pretty funny.

Milo asks if he can watch a movie. I tell him I'm sorry, we can't. He insists. "On your computer." At his cousins' house, he got to watch a lot of movies.

"There isn't any computer, honey. Somebody stole it." I play over and over the things I should have done. So many things. Back it up. Print it out. E-mail it to myself. Hide the computers. Take them with us. Take them to Jacob's house. *Lock the darn window.* The options play and replay, but it's too late for me to accomplish any of them. There are an infinite number of things I could have done. But I can't make any of them real.

We are outside playing Frisbee and have just eaten the single strawberry off of our first-year strawberry plants, when the junkies pull up in an unfamiliar car. The two of them, without the baby. I place myself directly on the pebbled path, squaring my shoulders toward her. I don't want to fight. I just want her to see me. I want her to see me, and I want to see her. But she just stumbles past. There is no spark of recognition in her eyes. Their faces register nothing at all. No grief. No guilt. No joy.

If it was them, it wasn't really them, I tell Amy on the phone that night. Their addiction has taken everything from them. I'm convinced they're not even human anymore.

But I am wrong about this, as I am so often wrong about everything that matters. Weeks later after I return from Nicaragua, when I am sure it was her because she got her picture taken by a security camera using my stolen credit card and before federal agents come to take her away on an unrelated and much more serious charge, we will hear one of her dogs crying. We will hear whining that doesn't stop all night, and then we will see her loading an old, crippled dog into the back of her car, tears running down her face, smearing the thick lines of black makeup. She will look like anybody else who has ever loved a dog.

Her companion, the one the Boston city cop will call "the skinny kid from Southie," will wait for her and lean on the back of our car and glance restlessly through our windows as if he'd rather be stealing something. I will know then that they are every bit as human as the rest of us. And I will cry for her, for her and her two-year-old son. I will cry for this whole godforsaken broken world and for the sky that fails to shelter us.

But at this moment, with the Frisbee loose in my hand and my feet on the loose pebbles of the walk, I watch them walking up the stairs, and in their dead, flat arrogance I do not see people. I see patterns of living things in dotted lines, unfinished, not ready to be cut out. I see the virus of fear and greed trying to replicate itself. I am looking for shelter. I can't help but ask God if there wasn't some way to soften my heart without crushing it.

I am sure now, I tell Nick, that we should move away from the East Coast. "We were never meant to live out here. I can't even go to sleep in this house. Can we at least think about it?"

Nick has little to offer. As the crises mount, one on top of another, he turns yet further into himself, becoming numb and mechanical because that's the only way to maintain functionality. I should be sorry just for asking. Unlike my husband and two tiny children, I don't have to sleep in this house right now because I am leaving very early in the morning to go to Nicaragua.

It's hard to even imagine going to sleep, with adrenaline coming and adrenaline going, the latter for my first trip into the equatorial unknown and the former for an intruder in my house. I am still wide awake at one o'clock when I hear a car alarm sound and a low whistle. I watch at the window as she comes down the stairs with the hooded sweatshirt drowning her face, as if that could hide the distinctive hunch in her shoulders or the hitch in her gait. She goes to the window of an idling car, makes an exchange there, and returns. I stand in the shadows, willing myself night vision, willing myself the ability to see lightness in the dark.

I am still awake, watching the red numbers change on the clock, when the alarm goes off. The kids are cheerful not because they aren't sleepy, but because it is such an adventure to get out of bed in the middle of the night. At the airport I get out of the car quickly because I think they will cry, and I don't want to make things any harder for Nick than they have to be. But as I walk away, I look back to imprint their faces in my mind, just as they were at that moment, curious and sleepy and starting to get a little worried in their car seats, because I know that I will miss them more than they will miss me.

The journey to Nicaragua is a little shorter than the one to Boise, but it feels long because I have so many things to worry about. I close my eyes in my aisle seat and see the tumors closing in on my husband's mother's breath; I imagine the phone call in which I will hear that she is dying; I imagine that it will happen while I am on the wrong side of the equator. I change the channel in my mind, but then I see a junkie crawling in through the bathroom window to steal my computer, with her hooded sweatshirt casting a deep shadow on her face. My eyes burst open, and I grab for the tiny TV screen. I watch it all the way to Nicaragua without sound. It annoys me that I am watching. It isn't until we have almost arrived, when others on the plane are standing up in the aisles to point out the view of Lake Managua, that I realize it is possible to use the buttons on the side of the television screen to turn it off.

I am traveling with three people from my church. They all speak Spanish to varying degrees. They have all been here before, all more than once, to visit this sister community out in the countryside of Nicaragua. In bits and pieces they explain to me that we are going first to the capital city of Managua to meet with the organization that hires our translators and provides us with clean water and carries our letters. There we will have an orientation in which I will be educated in all the things I need to know before we travel together to the rural village.

For the first half a day we are there, I don't understand anything. I ask for a telephone. I talk to Nick, who speaks only in English, which is strangely surprising. I am relieved even before I hear the news. His mother has no new tumors. Her disease is still very likely fatal, but she has some time.

I am shown to my room, which I share with two of my companions from Boston and three women from the village. I struggle to learn their names, turning the unfamiliar sounds over and over on my tongue.

Then darkness falls, and I can't make conversation, and my needy little children are a quarter of a world away from me. I have nothing else to do but sleep. I lie down among strangers, in a pretty bed by the garden, in the peace of the gathering night. And I sleep the sleep of a child.

I still am walking like a child with more confusion than anything else when we get on the bus for our first field trip. The four Americans are surrounded by Nicaraguans from our sister church in the village. We are all going together to visit another sister church here in the capital city of Managua. I've been told that the two communities are close, and they are looking forward to spending time together. I imagine little cups of juice and cocktail napkins.

When we arrive, there are chairs in a circle. We sit down and, after a brief and formal introduction, people start talking about the Sandanista revolution of 1979. There are no cocktail napkins. They talk about the fight for freedom, how they remember it, how they took back their city from a dictator who burned villages and cut down their children in the streets. They talk about the inspiration of the *campesino* Jesus, who inspires the people to resist the injustice of oppression. We hear stories of this very church, how they gathered as a rebel safe house against the will of their priest, and their priest locked them out, but they cut the lock and took back their building and didn't feel a bit guilty about it because they were the ones who built it with their own hands.

I have said little and understood less when our guide suggests we all break up into small groups so we can get into some really satisfying conversation. I think finally we're going to get to the cocktail napkins and the juice. I'm still expecting somebody somewhere to talk to me about the weather when a woman named Tatiana looks me dead in the eyes and says, "What are you doing about the problem of immigration in the United States?"

I stammer. What does she mean, what am I doing? What am I supposed to be doing? Who does this woman think I am? I scramble for something to say. There was my heart's discovery of the field workers in rural Idaho, but that was quickly startled from my mind by the illness of my husband's mother. I did go once with other Boston activists to a sit-in on the steps of the Massachusetts State House, protesting an "immigration crackdown" slipped into the budget bill.

I tell this story now to the woman named Tatiana. I brought coffee cake to the sit-in, although I remember someone saying to me afterward, with a mix of incredulity and disdain, "You brought coffee cake to a sit-in?" I don't know. I thought that if I were a college student sleeping outside for a week I would probably like some coffee cake, maybe with a lot of butter, maybe with a lot of brown sugar sprinkled over the top. I did what I could think of to do. I tried to bring some comfort.

Tatiana nods. She is satisfied. "This is a very difficult problem," she says. Her English is almost perfect. The few imperfections only make it more intense. She goes on to tell us that she is disappointed in the North American president because of what he has done in Honduras. I blink. Honduras. I don't have any idea what our president has been doing there.

Is this why I came down here? To Central America? To find out what my president, whom I elected, is doing on other continents in his spare time?

On the way back to the compound, I ask a couple people about Honduras, and a little bit at a time I hear a story of a military coup and our response, allegedly in the direction away from justice and human rights. I know nothing about this situation. Every little thing, to me, is an allegation. But I will not quickly forget the vision of a woman who said to me, "I am disappointed," while looking for all the world like a mother who has just discovered that her child has trashed the house.

I am disappointed too. I am disappointed that I have not shown up to eat at this table. I am in relationship with these people—by our history, by our economics, by our governments, by our shared humanity—and I have been oblivious to the nature of our dialogue. I can't even use my Year Without Internet as an excuse. This coup was in September of 2009, during a time when I was functioning almost exclusively online and would have described myself as well informed. I certainly was reading an awful lot of something.

There are so many little countries in the world! How can we possibly know what our government is doing in every single one of them? It's overwhelming, being the child of an imperial power. It is overwhelming, carrying the weight of all our power and our wealth.

There are two more days of orientation in the capital city. I am not learning so much as I am unlearning. It is my first unprotected and unmoderated view of poverty in another country, and it takes me apart, like a puzzle, right down to the pieces. We walk by families living in shanties made of cardboard and corrugated metal. The curls of smoke indicate cooking fires. Little children stare at us. I'm supposed to be taking pictures but I can't. My camera is a manual focus, and I can't get my arms to stop shaking.

Our translators are very excited to bring us to meet a group of activist youth in a poor neighborhood. We are told they are inspiring. When we arrive, they are sitting in chairs or standing under the edge of a pavilion, very close to one another. One is pregnant, and she is constantly being touched. Her friends massage her shoulders and her hands. I can't focus on anything. Somewhere nearby is the noise of children drumming. The heat. The simultaneous translation. I float halfway out of the session, half out of my body, until I hear one of my companions asking the young people if they have ever considered emigrating, leaving Nicaragua.

There is a ripple of glances and grimaces. My friend has struck something that rings. I want as much as the sharp-voiced Tatiana, or anyone, to know what I can do about the problem of immigration. I know that I'm about to find out more than I have ever wanted to know, and I grasp a notebook for security.

The first to speak is a young man. I can understand some of what he says not because my hurried Spanish lessons ever took, but because his face and hands are so expressive. The translation is clear and complete and not simultaneous. I write down every single word.

"Yes, I have thought about it. It is really difficult for us to find work. Then if we do find work, it is a job with a low salary. It is not enough to pay for all our needs in the home, not to think of university. And if your mother is single, you learn that you can't think of her providing for you, but you have to provide for her."

I am using the shorthand that I learned as a stage manager in my first real job out of college, writing down stage directions as fast as I could for unpredictable stage directors. The pregnant woman extricates her hands from their massage. She pauses for translation. *New paragraph.*

"The answer is not simple. I have many close friends who have emigrated, but personally I have never wanted to. I don't want to go just to earn more money. My country has responded to the most important needs that I have. In another country I have no idea what I would be exposed to. There have been cases of racism and violence, things we hear on the news or see on TV. I've never thought about emigrating long because in spite of poverty, I also think that in my country, what we really need, is here. The values that have been taught to me. I don't know if I would find that in another country. I'd like to go and visit, but I don't want to move, to go and work, to be a slave in another country. Here people work eight hours a day. In the US, they work long hours, sometimes more than one job. There is no time to have this kind of a space that we are having right now."

I'm almost out of breath trying to capture it. I want to get it exactly right, exactly as it was said, because the wise Madonna is right: in my life there is no space like this, not unless you go for a Year Without the Internet, and even then . . . I have only this moment, which I have earned by dropping out and opting out and losing everything and having no excuses not to come here. I want to put a net around it and force it into a notebook and stuff it in my luggage and drag it home.

New voice. New paragraph.

"I have had friends and close family members who have emigrated. They have suffered just in the travel to get there. It is not necessary. We are poor; that is true. My father complains we always have rice and beans. [*Laughter.*] But that is not the most important thing."

New paragraph.

"I have to admit I have thought about leaving. I've thought, *I've got to go.* But I also think I'm not going to buy a solution for everything by leaving. When I leave, my efforts, my strengths, my self-esteem, my values—these I will have to sacrifice. Why don't I stay and contribute to my own country, not spend my effort to fill someone else's pockets? Why don't I give what I can give of myself to my own people?"

The last to speak is a young man hovering at the back of the group that is spilling out from under the shade of the pavilion. "I'm kind of waiting to go. Supposedly for the same situation, I'm going to be leaving. Sometimes when I think about it, I actually want to just cry."

I lift my head quickly to read the young man's expression. But it is too late. What I have just heard is the translation, the echo. For him, the expression of grief and loss has already passed.

Finally, we are considered ready for our homestays in the village. As we ride in a bus going north along the Pan American Highway, I listen to the young women laughing in the seats behind me. They sound exactly like my niece and her friends, except that they are speaking a language I don't know, and they peel mangoes with their teeth.

Along the way we are joined by another translator. She is very thin and very beautiful and has a beautiful singing voice, which is a detail I can't miss because she is sitting right beside me, singing along to all the pop songs on the radio. She munches on something totally toxic and bright orange that comes in a crinkly foil bag. My head turns toward the sound, and she offers me one, and I say, "No, thank you," at which point she makes a face as if she might want to tell me something.

I know enough to know that I just made a mistake. I apologize, and she looks relieved and says that, yes, I should know that it isn't culturally acceptable in Nicaragua to refuse a gift. In other words, it wasn't okay for me to say, "No, thank you," to the offer of Cheetos. You can say, "*Sólo una gota,*" she says, using all ten of her fingers to make an extravagant gesture of smallness. "Just a drop."

I apologize again and look out the window. The road drops away into dirt and rocks. There is a river. We drive right across a shallow part. When we pull into the village, my companions are caught in a sea of warm hugs and recognition, while I have social anxiety and a wary eye out for any approaching Cheetos.

But then the beautiful singing translator walks with me into the church, where we sit in plastic chairs with our backs to the cool gray walls.

The village women come in too and sit and lean back into the hard plastic, their hands loose on their laps, and they begin to sing. To me it is an unearthly sound. I think that all the imaginings I have ever had of an angelic choir were not very well informed. Now I know that the angels will sing like this, in low voices, from their bellies and their chests, building a resonance that shakes the rib cage and loosens the guarded heart. At the first vibration I start crying, and I can't stop. The translator asks me in English if I'm okay. I say yes, I'm okay. I don't have any idea what's going on, but I know it is okay.

After the songs there is a ritual welcome. It is emotional and poetic and theatrical, like the Latin American poets who seem so audacious and overstated next to the stuffy Puritans of my own heritage. I realize that I am sitting with an entire room full of people who would make grand sweeping statements about the soul and use the word "seeking" in casual conversation. If I knew anything at all about the language or the culture, or how to survive this heat, I would think that I had finally come home.

I stand up when it is my turn to express gratitude, and I *shush* the voices of those sour-faced Puritans, and I just let my cheesy dramatic self go to town. Without a shred of fear or hesitation, I tell a room full of brown-skinned strangers that I want them to know why I've been crying. This is my first time in Nicaragua, and my heart is breaking. It is breaking open to make room for all this love. On the way here, on the bus, I had felt shame for my failures and the failures of my country, for how little I understood and for how much I have failed to be present to our shared humanity. But in this room, I tell them, my spirit is at rest. I thank God for bringing each one of them into my life today.

They nod, wisely, as if what I have to say is perfectly appropriate and not at all overkill. Maybe there was judicious editing on the part of the translator, who is also the facilitator of our discussions and who has twin backgrounds in faith and popular education. Or maybe she didn't mess with it at all, and I really did find the dish of grace I've been looking for.

I try to hold on to this. I write it down in my notebook. I am afraid that this is never going to happen to me again, that I can give out undiluted every drop of what I'm feeling and have not a single person roll their eyes.

We are ushered out of the church and into people's homes. I am abandoned by my translator and left to sit alone with an old man in a kitchen while he shells the beans and recites the names of baseball teams, looking at me for signs of recognition.

As a gesture of respect, I have been placed in one of the most substantial homes in the community, with a second house in the back, and many cows, and electricity from a wire hung across the ceiling.

The stove is an adobe oven with a wood fire. My hosts bring water in plastic buckets from the well. The pig wanders at will. The kitchen has two doorways, but no doors. When the beautiful singing translator comes back to help me get through dinner, I ask if I can help shell the beans. They allow me, with indulgent smiles. The matriarch announces with a grin that I am earning my right to have dinner.

I say, "I hope not. I won't get very much dinner," and they laugh. They are satisfied with me.

After dinner I am shown to my room, which is full of bats. They hang from the ceiling, their thumbs folded neatly into their armpits. But I have too little strength for fear and I sleep hard, like a child, and wake up early to the sound of the cows and the roosters. I have no idea what time it is or at what time it is appropriate to go to the kitchen or ask for coffee. I am totally dependent on the care and compassion of my hosts. I can't communicate. I can't feed myself. I can't draw my own water or wash my own clothes. I can't even sneak out to a café or store to use money to take care of my needs. I can only rest in total dependency.

I do get coffee. And a shower. And clean clothes. Then I meet Emma, a sophomore in college who speaks lovely, fluent Spanish. We are helping to organize a fund-raising event for the building of a new church, and we talk about this project as we count tiny slips of paper for the raffle. Emma first came to this village when she was thirteen years old. She tells me that she thinks this is where God is. Not just in Nicaragua, but in any place where we become small and helpless and the ego starves as we give others the gift of our mutual dependence. She takes her shoes off here. This is holy ground.

That day two different people tell me, smiling, that I am like Jesus' disciples, because I left my family behind to take a pilgrimage. The matriarch of my homestay quotes the Gospels over lunch. She says I have followed the command, "Take up my cross and follow me."

I find this assertion strange and strangely healing. In the US I am still a border Christian, still an occupant of the fringe. I am one who sees all the things my mother didn't see—collective memories of Christian bigotry, our connections to imperialism, the ways our faith communities have perpetrated and tolerated harm. I do not quote the Gospels over lunch.

But here the gospel is a part of the culture. Interwoven. The gospel itself trumps its social context. And Christ wins. I am as a child, relearning the deep simplicity of the faith of a child. It is as if some gentle hand is reaching into the wound of my dotted-line faith journey and closing the gaps, letting a strong faith begin to lift out the deep tangles in mine.

On Sunday we go on retreat. Members of the Church of the Poor leave their kitchens and their crops to circle with us under the mango trees, where we have conversations about faith and miracles and the hopes and dreams of both communities. In the early afternoon we leave the grove of mango trees and go into the church, because everyone except for me can tell by looking at the sky that it is about to rain.

We sing, and again the pitch of the song shakes things loose in my chest. There is a Scripture from Isaiah about water in the desert, and the rain beats heavy on the roof as the Delegate of the Word invites us all to speak from our hearts in response to the Word. Emma is one of the first to speak. She speaks in Spanish, but I hear in the translation that she is talking about abundance, a sudden abundance of water falling from above. "Sometimes, suddenly," she says, "there is so much."

At the end of the service we stand and sing, *"La paz, la paz, es fruta de la justicia,"* as a little girl walks around the circle with a pine needle basket. Someone puts in a coin: one cordoba. Someone else puts in another coin: two cordobas. I am frightened of carrying money, for reasons I am afraid to articulate, so I have nothing in my pockets to give. But the North American woman standing next to me reaches into her cargo pants and drops into the basket a 20-cordoba bill. The little girl forgets her charge completely and runs back to show her grandmother what bounty has fallen into her basket. Twenty cordobas. By the exchange rate, in US currency, one dollar.

Sometimes, suddenly, there is so much.

It is nearly time to go. We end with the most practical discussions, the conversations about the material support we offer, money for the building of a new church. The leaders explain to us that their long-term goal is to stop emigration, to stop their young people from leaving. The sheer naïveté of the goal makes me wonder again what it is that makes anyone stand up to their Goliath. But hope always shows up like this, looking ridiculous and childlike against the sheer size of the opposition.

As we make our rounds of good-byes, one of the women has made some cookies and is, I think, offering for me to buy them. But the opportunity is veiled by pride, perhaps, or wanting not to offend me, or by something else. I struggle to interpret what's expected. Her three-year-old daughter watches me as I eat the sweet banana that her mother has insisted that I take, and although I cringe with the guilt and the worry, I know better now than to ever say, "No, thank you."

As I walk away from the house, the little girl is still watching me. She is standing in the doorway like a picture in *National Geographic*. I have bought a handful of cookies for six cordobas, what in US currency is six nickels or three dimes. I can't yet predict the letter we will receive a few months later, telling us that this particular woman has tried and failed to emigrate to Europe, trying to go to another country to work, to send money back to the wide-eyed child in the doorway. But already I can't understand why I didn't buy every cookie she had. Who cares whether or not I like cookies. How could I miss the opportunity to leave behind a little bit more of what I have?

On our way back to Managua, I begin to cry quietly, sitting on this bus on our cracked vinyl seat hurtling through space. If I go back West, to the mountains that I don't know why I ever left, to undo my own emigration toward economic opportunity, if I do that, I will leave behind the church where I have been baptized. I will leave behind the city of Boston, this *hermanamiento*, this sister relationship with a community in Nicaragua, this facilitation that made it possible for a skittish traveler like me to begin to see the world this way. This bus seat, this church, this village, and this Nicaragua will be just one more place that I have moved through, like any other soul in this rootless generation, gathering up from each place what it has to offer and moving on.

The next morning we make a farewell visit to the market, and I understand that the others are buying gifts to take home. The context shifts again, as if we have been here all this time for our own purposes instead of God's. The beggar children press their reed creations on us, touching our hands and our bags, following us out to our car with their open hands, saying perhaps the only English words they know. "Money, please. Money, please." I give the rest of my Nicaraguan currency—all change—to a man who comes up at a stoplight to wash the car windows. At the next stoplight, when another man comes up to wash the car windows, I show him my empty hands.

There is a bitter taste in the air when we walk out of the plane in Houston. I want to see my children. It is physical, the way I miss my children. But I don't have to hear Emma disagreeing with her mother over the purchase of a plastic water bottle to know that another gap has closed. We have returned to the land of our fathers, and our sins are here to meet us at the door.

PART FOUR

the *Fog*

Ten

The Dragon

My children are waiting for me near the baggage claim. Milo runs across the shiny floor, his arms flying side to side, crying, "Mama! Mama!" It is a movie-quality homecoming. We're completely adorable.

But then we get into our car, and after a miserable hour on the freeway, I feel disoriented and confused. Our home seems too big, too full. I don't know where all this stuff came from or what it's for. I'm interpreting things too slowly, following my own body from behind. This is a reverse culture shock.

Fortunately for me, the fog has no real-world consequences. Neither of my children needs anything from me right at the moment, having become accustomed, apparently, to my absence. And my husband doesn't need anything from me right now either, since he is giving his full attention to the Internet.

Oh, Internet. Internet. Internet! I should have given my neighbors that banana bread. At some unknown point in the last six months, a neighbor has installed a wireless router with no security. And while I was in Nicaragua, having my heart broken open to make room for so much love, my husband was sitting here in this apartment, bored enough to get on the half-broken computer that wasn't stolen because you would have to pay someone to take it, patient enough to endure its Paleolithic time signature, and lonely enough—even after the years of resistance to social networking—to set up his first profile page on Facebook.

I stare at my husband for a moment. And scratch my nose. It is August in Boston, but it feels like a balmy spring in comparison to *el campo*. I open a bag and start unpacking my notebooks. There is a silver dragon charm sitting on my desk. I pick it up and turn it over in my hands.

"How did this get here?"

Nick looks up from where he is typing by hunt and peck on the broken keyboard. "Milo found it. I told him to put it there. It's yours, isn't it?"

"No." This dragon is not mine, nor would I wear it. But I have seen it, in passing, tied by a black cord to another woman's neck. I picture my toddler son carrying it, unsuspectingly, from wherever it was he found it, and I shudder.

How much time did she spend in my apartment? Sitting on my couches? Rifling through my drawers? Long enough to lose a necklace? When I tell Emily about it later, she says, "What was she doing, trying on your clothes?"

We call our detective. He sends one of his detective buddies, who puts the dragon in a little plastic baggie and swaggers down the porch steps with it. He talks like a Boston cop right out of a movie, identifying the item as some kind of evidence, but remaining incredibly unconvincing regarding what on earth he is going to do with it. I immediately regret that I didn't keep the dragon for myself, as some kind of talisman.

Jacob comes over. He is somewhat alarmed at all the trauma we've been through and is making a special effort to take care of me.

We talk about the break-in and the progress of the investigation. Nick explains that there was security camera footage taken at a big box store of the junkie from upstairs using my credit card, but it turns out that is not useful as evidence that she broke into our house, because she could have just picked the credit card up off the street. Our detective doesn't think we have much of anything to go on.

I explain to Jacob that I am coming to understand the whole theft as a physical expression of my altered value system. As a result of my year without the Internet, I had become ambivalent about my computer, I tell him. I had come to believe that my computer was a thing I didn't really want in my life. I was failing to make decisions with my computer's best interests in mind.

Jacob says, "Oh, Esther, that isn't what happened. Sometimes people get robbed."

I liked my version better. I sulk.

In the morning I make a pan of muffins and wrap them up in tin foil and a thin red ribbon left over from last Christmas. For that whole strange wrinkle in time that we were in Boise—while I was witnessing an anti-drug campaign and the mortality of someone I love, and two junkies were destroying nine months' worth of my life's work on a computer they could sell for maybe fifty bucks—all that time the junkie's mom was watering my garden. I had asked her to. I had promised to bake her something in return. She likes the bread we make, half wheat and half white flour. But the little boy likes my muffins.

I carry the silver crinkly bundle up the back stairs and knock on the door. No one answers my knock, which doesn't surprise me. I speak into the heavy thrice-locked kitchen door. "It's just me. I made you some muffins." She opens the door, still looking suspicious. "These are for you. For watering my garden."

She looks past me. I press them into her hands. She nods but still says nothing. I trot back down the back stairs, suppressing the urge to run until I am safely through my own kitchen door, punching down bread dough for supper with Jacob.

I have an undeniably bragging tone in my voice a few hours later as I am pulling the finished bread loaves from the oven. I am relating to Jacob how I had the strength of character to give my neighbor the promised baked goods, even under these tense circumstances.

He leans against the counter, his arms folded, and speaks with even more precision than usual. "Esther, I'm not sure that it's a good idea to give gifts to people who steal from you. You might be setting yourself up as a victim."

I tip out the bread a bit more violently than I need to. I feel suddenly, irrationally that I would do anything to prove him wrong. I can't control what my neighbors do—not the junkie, not her boyfriend, not the mother who tries to keep her daughter from leaving in the middle of the night. But there is one thing that I can control, and that's what I do. I can control whether I speak into this situation in fear . . . or in love. This is the only choice I really get to make.

Jacob doesn't understand me. I am not speaking clearly. It doesn't come out as well as it does in my head. And Jacob is already worried about me. He wants to guide me back into the center. I want to drive him out to the edge. He talks. I talk. We hear ourselves talking. We miss each other in the air.

Nick is ignoring the entire conversation. He is running a different tape. He is convinced that our computers are still upstairs right now. And that while he is struggling to update his Facebook status with the missing spacebar and backspace keys, they are upstairs drafting on his computer with his AutoCAD or retouching photos with his Photoshop.

Also, this week his mother is starting radiation.

This is how Bernie's cancer treatment goes: radiation first, then chemotherapy. The amount and schedule of both is not in response to the cancer, but set in advance, because there is only so much radiation that the human body can be expected to endure without permanent damage, and that is precisely the quantity they intend to administer. We hope it kills the cancer instead of killing her. I keep asking Nick about the details of a move out West, our escape route, our Exodus, but the only voyage he can manage is a simple visit, even that six weeks away, to hang out with his mom during a round of chemotherapy.

Until then, he works. The fall season at his work is getting under way, the work days again becoming long, the pressure high. We have less time to talk. There is his world, of work and computers and purchasing materials and rolling his eyes at that strange class of creatures who call themselves professional artists. And then there is my world, of late summer heat and humidity and diapers and naps and pan after pan of muffins and the silence of the early-morning fog rolling in off the bay.

The junkies have installed a camera on the front of the house, which we can only assume is recording us as we walk to the car to do our grocery shopping, or play Frisbee on our little patch of yard between the raised beds, or take our children in a homemade wagon to the beach. It does not, however, record what must be their transactions with a drug dealer, who pulls up in a shiny car just past our house, sometimes now more than once a day.

I've lost perspective on the Year Without Internet. It seems it would be effortless just to let it go. As I am trying to type up my notes that I took in Nicaragua on a broken computer, missing several keys, I notice that my computer is connected to Wi-Fi, probably from upstairs. The Web browser is already launched.

There is an arrow underneath the icon. All I would have to do is click once.

I go back to my transcription. *Click click click. Click click click.* I am typing, slowly, and reading the words out of my notebook, spoken by a young man in the heat against the sound of children drumming. *"I have to admit I have thought about leaving. I've thought, I've got to go. But I also think I'm not going to buy a solution for everything by leaving. When I leave, my efforts, my strengths, my self-esteem, my values—these I will have to sacrifice. Why don't I stay and contribute to my own country . . . to my own people?"*

Why does it seem like the young man is talking right to me?

I pick up the phone and call Amy in California. I ask her if she will go on my blog, or on my Facebook page, or anywhere else that she thinks anybody will remember me—does anyone remember me?—and try to find someone who has an opinion about whether I should finish out the year without Internet. I tell her that I just don't have the motivation to do it by myself. I'm too depressed, too isolated, too confused. If I'm going to rewrite it, I need to know that somebody remembers me. I need to know that somebody out there cares.

Missy calls right away. She says she heard from Amy what's going on, and she wants me to know that she totally agrees with me. She doesn't think I need to do a whole year. If I've learned what I needed to learn, then I could just be done now and save myself from this hard time. Then I could get back to the Internet tomorrow and see all the cute videos of her four-year-old daughter that she has been posting on Facebook.

I grin in spite of myself. "How is she?"

"She's great," Missy says. "Parenting is getting better." She explains that they have been turning off the television more and that seems to be helping to calm down the wild pace of their house, in which both parents work and freelance in the creative life. Missy explains that if the TV is turned off, Lydia can go into a state of imaginative play, which actually keeps her more occupied and happy and lets Missy get more of her own work done.

"Missy!" I exclaim. "Do you hear what you're saying to me?" She and I talked a lot before about why I don't let my kids watch TV, and although Missy never agreed with me before, she appears to have just essentially restated my central argument. Is she admitting to me, her crazy opt-out disappearing friend, that her life has been somehow enriched by exposure to my hard-headed habits of resistance?

"Mmm . . . yeah."

"Oh, Missy." I sigh. "You aren't doing a very good job of convincing me to quit my experiment."

"I know," she says, "but I've gotta try. I'm on Facebook all the time, and I miss you."

I decide that I can make the year after all. I take out my notebook, with a flash of that old idea that I'll get back to making ingenious and insightful discoveries about life without the Internet. But all I find myself writing down is description after description of the junkies upstairs. I capture every detail, their patterns of movement, the timing of the drug dealers who come to the house at least once a day, their license plate numbers.

One afternoon I lean against the dining room window with my digital camera and take a picture, which is dramatic, because somehow the driver sees me—or sees the flash?—and he suddenly peels out in reverse and the tires squeal. My picture has motion streaks in it.

Jacob says, "Wait. You took a picture?"

"Yeah."

"And they saw you?"

"I think so."

"Esther. Don't you think that's dangerous?"

"Oh, Jacob . . . I don't know. Which part is dangerous? The part where I try to be a responsible citizen? Or the part where I live here?"

But then I don't know. Maybe my brother is right. Maybe it does take more than forgiveness to turn criminals into friends. Maybe the strong arm of the law is helpful too. I am just about to call our detective and offer up all the pictures and the notes when a Quincy police car comes to a stop in front of our house and sticks around. Half an hour later there is a Boston cop as well. I call Amy back in California and say, "Dude." (This is an act of rebellion in itself. Nobody in Boston ever says "dude.")

"Dude," I say to Amy, "I think there is a police stakeout happening right now. In front of my house."

"Dude," she answers back. "That is crazy. Let me know what happens."

But what happens next, and for the entire afternoon, is absolutely nothing. I guess this is the part they cut out of the action movies. Nothing happens until just before dark when a big black SUV pulls up across the street and lets out some crazy fit-looking men with short haircuts and ID tags. But I'm not on the phone with Amy anymore, and my husband is back to his crazy hours at work, so if I'm going to make any exclamations, I have to make them to the cat.

"Chet, I'm pretty sure those are federal agents."

The G-men gather in a loose knot around our gate. They look nonchalant, as if my front walk just happened to be a nice place to gather and chat about the weather. Maybe they're admiring my pepper plants. Maybe they're rooting for that one little cucumber vine. I put my shoes on and go out and offer them coffee and vegan chocolate cake. I'm an equal-opportunity baker. But they are not from Nicaragua, and they turn me down. I turn to the G-man with the impossibly smooth and well-defined pectoral muscles and tell him about some additional objects that we have discovered missing from our house, especially the bright red change bucket. It seems like that would be lying around and easy to spot. He knits his brows together and sticks out his lips. The Quincy cop tells me to go inside and go to bed.

And that's what I do. That's exactly how old and boring I am. I go to bed. My children are already in bed. My husband comes home from work and he goes to bed too, and we all sleep right through until early the next morning. I hear voices and, leaning against the glass, I watch the junkie boyfriend get moved out. His bags loaded into the car, his suddenly possessive good-bye hug to the little boy, the crimping fierce look of anger on the grandma's face. I don't know where they took the junkie herself. I don't know who took the camera off the front of the house or who, if anyone, will ever watch the footage of me playing Frisbee in my yard and picking strawberries.

In the middle of the day, Nick calls our detective and gets the news. The whole stakeout, it turns out, was a bust. The whole time she wasn't home. They picked her up somewhere else and searched the house without resistance. And in what Nick describes as "colorful language," the detective told Nick that he didn't know about the stakeout. The federal agents were after her for a completely unrelated charge—alleged armed robbery of a bank in Connecticut—and by a common case of crossed wires, none of the officers who gathered around our gate—not the Quincy cop, nor the Boston cop, nor the G-man with the impossibly smooth pectoral muscles—were told that the nosy neighbor with the chocolate cake had any legitimate interest in the case.

They didn't know about our stolen laptops. They didn't know to even look for our laptops. They searched the place without searching for our laptops, and now there isn't a chance to search again. Nick is angry. I'm just stunned. I'm too stunned to know what I feel about this or about anything else under the sun. The detective says our case is closed. He says she probably didn't have the laptops anymore anyway. She probably sold them right away for fifty bucks. We shouldn't bother to call him anymore.

I keep coming back to the same passage in the Bible. The blind man asks Jesus for a miracle. Jesus makes a mud out of spit and dirt and rubs it on the blind man's eyes. Then he says, "Go wash in the pool." But I'm stuck partway through. I keep thinking, What kind of a Savior is this? Who puts mud on my face and leaves me here?

It's late August in Boston. Summer is just now sliding toward fall. The humidity is like a second skin. I don't know where my feet are. I start writing a letter every day. I write letters to fight the depression. I write letters to give some structure to my life. I write them by hand because I can't stand the stupid broken computer. I write letters to pretty much everybody I know, but especially to people with whom I have had some kind of correspondence over the last nine months. I tell them what happened. Sometimes I make an open plea for help. I ask for community, for connection, for dialogue and friendship. I ask people to laugh at my stupid jokes. I write the story of what happened to my computer over and over again. My project got stolen, I say. My whole project is gone. I ask my friends if they have kept my letters and, if so, would they send me copies of them? I'm trying to keep a record of it, so this strange magic gap in my life doesn't disappear completely from memory.

Several people don't write back and never will. My feminist theater director friend, Kirsten Brandt, sends everything right away.

She says she has kept it in a file. I read my own words back to myself, and it feels strange, like hearing your own voice recorded. I didn't know my voice sounded so squeaky—and so young. Suddenly I wonder if the whole stolen manuscript sounded like that. Maybe I should be grateful to the woman from upstairs for stealing my amateur attempt. Maybe she was an angel after all who saved me from a terrible embarrassment.

I am holding one of these precious handwritten letters when I realize that I can tell it's about to rain. I don't know exactly how I know, but I know. It is about to rain that thick wet-towel rain that will tell me I have been in this part of the world for one whole turning of the seasons. I wipe my eyes with my fingertips and get up from my desk. I intend to get Milo out of the sandbox. I intend to be a responsible parent. But even though the first few drops are falling, he doesn't want to come inside. He is deep in play. The trucks, he tells me, are friends with each other. They're building something together. They're all getting wet. He's happy.

I haven't taken any time to work in the yard, not since I came back from Nicaragua, not since the junkie was taken away by federal agents. Our yard is still the second ugliest yard on the block. But the garden we planted is growing as best it can. The peppers are laden. The basil is lush. The first-year strawberry plants are green and alive. The jalapeno peppers haven't been harvested—I haven't paid any attention—and I realize that every single one of the peppers has a little bite taken out of it. Some squirrel neighbor has tasted every single one. What was he thinking, that maybe the next one wouldn't be so hot? Or maybe the next one?

Finally I look at the cucumber plant, the only one of the four plants my sister picked out for me to plant that wasn't uprooted or chopped off. And there's a cucumber. Growing on the vine. One little cucumber. It's right there.

I can't bear it, suddenly, that this is true. Things grow again.

Milo is just as excited about the growing cucumber as I am. He squats in the dirt under the wring-out-a-towel rain and looks at it, reverently, without touching. A few days later, on the last day of August, he will have a birthday and turn three years old. On that day we will run our old video camera, the one that still takes a tape, while Milo trots down the porch stairs and picks his one special cucumber off the vine. His cousins will come from New York for the birthday celebration, and all day long I will serve salads of various kinds, and people will ask, "Is this the cucumber? Is this the one?"

I will have to go to bed immediately after dinner, overcome by my own ridiculousness. Because here I am, the daughter of a woman who wrote an entire book on food self-sufficiency, and I think I have just been saved by a single cucumber.

Boston is a whole city that begins again in September. My church begins to wake up from the sleepy summer. Programs begin again. Attendance rises. I go to every service. I go early and stay late. I don't know what it will take to fill the well again, to wet the dry places. But I'm trying.

I look for the feeling I found in Nicaragua, the feeling of intense meaning and togetherness with a group. I look for a place where forgiveness is tangible, where people come together to occupy a space of healing. I don't know where to find it or even exactly what it looks like. But I am wandering. Looking. Turning over stones.

The blind man asks Jesus for a miracle. Jesus makes a mud out of spit and dirt and rubs it on the blind man's eyes. Jesus says, "Go wash in the pool." The blind man says, "Dude, can't you see I'm blind? How am I supposed to find the pool?"

It is early on a Sunday morning when the fog finally begins to lift. I am doing a presentation at my church about the trip to Nicaragua. It is not a large group, but my hands shake anyway, from fear of public speaking. I fight through it, as I am so accustomed to do. I warn the listeners that I might cry, and indeed I do. I assign parts, and we read aloud my transcription that I typed out on the old broken computer. In our voices as mostly white and uniformly privileged citizens of the USA, we lift up the words of the Nicaraguan youth:

"I have to admit it, I have thought about leaving."

"Why don't I give what I can give of myself to my own people?"

"I am going to be leaving soon for Guatemala. Sometimes when I think about it, I want to just cry."

Others speak about their experiences. We read an e-mail from Emma, the sophomore in college who is back at school. And then it is my turn again, and I tell as quickly as I can the story about forgiveness. There is only one story about forgiveness. It is always the same story. It begins with crimes committed, man against man, human against human. I didn't know, I say. I keep repeating this. I didn't know. I couldn't even find Nicaragua on a map. I knew there were wars. I knew about that phrase "national security." But I didn't know what that really meant. I chose not to know.

But then, albeit mostly by accident, I turned. And all I had to do was turn. I looked back at the home I ran away from, my birthright, my capacity for communion with other human beings. And I was welcomed there in relationship with my brothers and sisters in Nicaragua. Like the prodigal son coming home, I was met on the way with songs and sweet bananas and Cheetos and a trip to the carnival.

Forgiveness is possible. A space opens up where before there was fear. Some measure of guilt can be replaced by an equal measure of solidarity. But there is a catch. If I want to keep this connection, I have to remain changed. If I want to keep this prize, I can never again say, "I didn't know." I can't say I didn't know about the sweatshops, where workers earn wages in pennies for clothing I buy in dollars. I can't say I didn't know about the banana pickers who weren't told that the wide green leaves were brushed with toxic chemicals and whose families were never yet compensated for their illnesses and deaths. I can never again say I don't know what we mean when we say we are "developing" the "undeveloped" world.

Jesus says to the blind man, "Go to the pool and wash." The man says, "I know, Jesus, you've been telling me this for years, but I tell you what, I've thought about it. And I'd rather stay blind."

Who knew that forgiveness would be so inextricable from loss?

After church I take the train home. I walk the half mile from the station, march through the gate, up the walk, and directly to Emily's organic orchid. I take the pile of one-hundred-dollar bills out from under the sack of dirt. I designate part to the church to pay back my plane fare to Nicaragua and then several more parts to organizations that do work I respect. We are still on our debt-end plan. I am still concerned about the future plane tickets to Boise and replacing our computers. There is no extra money to spare, but I can't not do this. I have to remain changed, even though I am back in this place—my too big, too full home, where mangoes are exotic and forgiveness is something we talk about on Sundays.

This is the one thing that I can do—unearth my buried money. And isn't it what Emma taught me, reading Isaiah in Spanish in a church with a leaky roof? "For I will pour water on the thirsty land, and streams on the dry ground."* There is a name for this. That name is abundance.

"Suddenly," she said, "there is so much."

---

* Isaiah 44:3.

The Dragon

Nick and I make pesto out of our own basil for dinner, and I find myself talking and talking and talking, like the waters, in this way too have finally risen over the banks. Nick is silent, as usual, but his silence has a quality of relief as he listens to me. We are picking up where we left off: conversations about integrity and self-reliance. I had faltered because it felt like we were moving in a direction away from everybody else. But now I realize that there is a bigger "everybody else." I realize that there is a whole, beautiful world of God's creation that has been waiting for me to stumble home.

All the steps are very small steps. No more bananas from the grocery store. No more coffee from the grocery store. I think about where things come from. I think about the straw hats in the fields. I try to understand how far back on the supply chain you have to go to find oppression, inhumanity, and injustice. Often, it isn't very far. I think about how to buy different things or how to make things myself. I think about how my friend Rick saw a woman in a cardboard sun hat, and this was his revelation: that if you really needed a hat, you could just make one.

My husband and I are moving in the same direction again. Finally, we are both fully engaged and fascinated by the same thing, which is figuring out what things we really need and making them ourselves. We go on a double date with old friends to an orchard to pick our own apples. We bring them home and make apple butter using a recipe in my mother's book. The whole house smells like spiced apples, and we don't buy bananas that week. In that moment, abundance and justice are somehow intertwined. Reading Simone Weil, I underline, "We have invented the distinction between justice and charity."[*]

---

[*] Simone Weil, *Waiting for God*, trans. Emma Craufurd (New York: Harper Perennial Modern Classics, 2009), 83.

Jesus makes sense to me in this, the bridge between justice and abundance. Jesus makes sense to me at the point of total transformation, where grace lifts the weight of self-hatred while paving the way to responsible action. I don't know if I dare say this out loud to anyone just yet, but Jesus makes sense to me in apples and handmade hats. It's a bridge I can put my feet on.

One night I come into the kitchen after the kids are in bed and Nick is sitting with his computer. I see that he is on Facebook, and I turn around to leave. He tells me to stay. I protest.

"It's okay. I'll go . . ."

"No," he says. "I'd rather be with you."

I melt. I am thirty-one years old. I have two children. And somebody just finally invited me to the prom.

So this is what it looks like, when joy creeps in. It collects in pools in the kitchen. I don't notice until I'm standing in it. I'm just stumbling around like normal, and then suddenly I'm standing in a pool of grace. I hear myself laughing. We have insane amounts of pesto. I'm making egg noodles from scratch. We're learning how to make our own cheese out of raw milk. I tell Nick that I think I feel like learning to juggle clubs, like clowns do in the circus, and he buys me a set of juggling clubs to learn on. I go out in the yard every day to practice. The neighbor in the giant pickup truck slows down and rolls down his window to watch me. I wave and grin. He waves back, tentatively, and watches as I try to set a rhythm with the clubs. I drop them every single time.

We tell the landlord we will stay at least until the spring.

I didn't notice when the summer ended and the fall began. The chill creeps. The colors at the farmers' market are less vibrant. Boxes and boxes and piles and piles of squash. I no longer judge a right or righteous purchase by the number of miles away or by a sticker on a label. Nor do I judge it by organic, or vegetarian, or vegan. I judge it by contact. I try to get myself face-to-face with the people who grow my food or, better yet, their children. I want to look them in the eyes and say thank you. I want to live the truth of abundance that I read in Scripture and saw with my own eyes in Central America and came again to believe in here because of one cucumber that grew against all odds.

It is here, at the farmers' market, that I am once again in Nicaragua, in the place of my helplessness. I cannot feed myself, not here any more than in a Third World country. I depend on others, notably the ones who know how to grow more than one cucumber per season, but I also depend on the earth itself. I depend on the gifts of what we sometimes call Creation, freely given. "What do you have that you did not receive?"* What do we have that is not given?

It falls from the sky.

The harvest does for me what the best of church can do for me. I cry purchasing sweet potatoes and green beans the way I cry during an old sweet hymn. I cry because this is just exactly how it ought to be: our sustenance passing from hand to hand, an unbroken chain, each intersection another chance to raise our voices and say thank you. I cry because the chain of human hands is so broken in so many places, and there are so many people falling off the ends. I cry because the whole image is so childish and naive, and I think I'm getting really foolish now. But I want to grow backward, like my grandma and Bob Dylan. I want to get younger so I can once again believe in the fairy tale of human interdependence. I cry because of the superhuman courage it takes to reach out my hand just to one person somewhere near me, to receive the gifts that are not theirs to give nor mine to steal.

---

* 1 Corinthians 4:7.

Finally, when I am back in my car where nobody can see me, I cry for my mother. I cry for my mother, Carla Emery, one of the founders and figures of the modern homesteading movement and a bastion of counterculture, standing behind a plastic table heavy laden with her books, with her wide smile at the end of a slow day starting to set like Jell-O, quivering at the edges.

I cry for my childhood, growing up in the fear of not making it, not making enough money for dinner, not making the rent, having to sleep in the car and wash our faces in public bathrooms, and the years I spent wondering why she bothered. Why, like those farmers who are always struggling, who are always losing their farms to the bank, why didn't she go and do something useful with her life, like write speeches for politicians—she would have been good at that!—or, better yet, get into the finance industry and specialize in hidden fees? My childhood could have been so much easier.

But the old farmers don't leave their farms until they have to. And my mother didn't either. She died on the road with her plastic table and her books in the back of the van. My mother, like the farmers, made her stand. She stood against the encroachment, against the forgetting, against the manufactured consumer-driven world. This is my inheritance. And I have come here to the farmers' market and to the Year Without Internet to claim it.

This is true. It's amazing and powerful and sometimes scary, but it's true. Things grow again.

Eleven

For Soul to Weep

*O*n the day my dad calls me on the phone, I am sitting at my desk, reading something about the Dalai Lama. This part is normal. The phone call is not normal. Not that I'm counting, but this is the second time in my adult life that my ephemeral, here-again, gone-again father has ever made a phone call to me unsolicited. What follows is one of the most genuine interactions we have ever had. My grandmother is dying, he tells me. Dying now, in her nursing home in northern Utah. He doesn't expect me to come. He sent an e-mail to the other kids, but he didn't think there was any other way to reach me except to call.

He's right. There is no other way to reach me except to call. I feel a twinge of guilt. How much easier it might have been for him to just send the e-mail, to not have to give breath to these words. His mother. Dying. I ask him if he is okay. I try to invite some conversation, but he doesn't bite. The funeral, he says, will wait until the following week. This weekend is the General Conference of the Church of Latter-day Saints. Everybody is busy. He hangs up the phone.

The day that I receive this phone call is a Tuesday. It is also the eighth anniversary of my wedding day. My father does not remember this, but Nick's father does and sends a card. What neither of our fathers remembers, or can remember, because nobody told them, is that today is also the second anniversary of the day that marriage fell apart.

I put the phone back on the charger base and go into the kitchen. The dishes are already done. I wonder how many of my brothers and sisters have checked their e-mail. I wonder which one I could call and what I would say. I wonder how soon someone will call me to tell me that my grandmother has actually died. Who will have that job? Will I know, somehow, across the distance? Will I feel it? Or will I be, as I so often am these days, the last one to know?

It is a Tuesday, and on Tuesday we go to the Goodwill. I pack the kids into the car, as usual, I drive, as usual, unload the kids, and I hold Milo's hand across the parking lot. I look through the books too, as usual. But the titles don't come into focus. I gather up some dust on my fingertips. Milo says to me, "Mama. Guitar. Can we buy it?"

I look over. The guitar is in the furniture section, leaning against a couch, so busted up it is almost unrecognizable. It only has three strings. "Guitar," I say to Milo. "You're right. Good word."

The price is $15.99. The checker is a pretty blonde woman who is pregnant. She shows me the price tag and says, "Is this okay?" By this she means, do you fully realize that you are about to pay $15.99 for a musical instrument that is very ugly and will never ever by any magic be made to sound good?

"I know," I answer, slightly groaning. But it's too late now. It has already happened. My son had an impulse. And I had neither the energy nor the wisdom to resist it. We are bringing home a broken, ugly guitar to a house where nobody can play it.

At home, Milo is more interested in his trucks. I find myself sitting with the broken guitar on my lap, left hand on the fret board, right hand on the strings. My father used to play "Froggy Went a Courtin'." I don't know if he knew how to play anything else. In my memory, he played like a cowboy, with his Levis and his belt buckle. He played the way you play when you've no company in the world but the sound of your own voice and the moon and the guitar.

Nick, wisely, does not purchase a gift to commemorate the day. He comes home with sober eyes and a bottle of wine. I tell him about the phone call. He nods. It can hardly add stress to an already stressful day. We sip our wine and stare at the broken guitar.

It is my idea, as these things always are, to make a list. "Honey, let's make a list of things we want to do this year. But let's make it a list of things we want to do together. It will be our anniversary present to each other."

"Okay."

We want to go sledding. We want to grow a better garden. We want to cook more. By the time we get to number eight, we are smiling again, sliding a little closer to each other on the couch. It is Nick's turn. He says, "Let's learn to play a song on the guitar."

I grin. Why not? We're not too old. It's not too late. Nick is the type who always should have known how to play the guitar. It fits with his whole lumberjack, strong, silent witty thing. We finish our list of ten and hang it up with a little sparkle and a little hope, even in the shadow of death. We will remember our eighth anniversary as our thrift store anniversary: the year we bought our marriage back from the donation bin.

Only a few days pass before I receive the phone call saying that my grandmother is dead. The funeral is on, as scheduled, in Utah. My dad will be there, along with his sister and a few more relatives we share. Jacob can't leave work. But I am going. If I can't go to my grandmother's funeral under my current circumstances—as an opt out, open space, no chains kind of spiritual seeker—it's because I never was going to go. I quickly arrange some babysitting and make a phone call to the airline to purchase tickets. And then for the second time this year, I head back to the Rocky Mountains where my bones were formed.

Once again, travel lifts me out of my responsibilities. I travel like a child. I can't even call to check on my family until I have arrived at my hotel room, met my sisters, and dialed the landline phone in my room.

Darkness draws into night as I stand arranging pictures of Grandma on a corkboard that we will bring with us to the Latter-day Saints church in the morning. I am mostly silent and listening, while my family all around me is talking, mostly about food. I wonder if I ever noticed that I come from a whole tribe of people who talk about food. No wonder my joys and my anxieties have both been trapped in it. Our roots run deep.

The casket is open. One of my sisters, who is a secular Buddhist, stands for a long time in front of it, staring into the face of a dead woman, doing the compassionate meditation practice she tells me is called Tonglen. Another sister, who is Mormon, like all our hosts, is invited to draw the veil. She cries a little. She pulls the gauzy fabric over Grandma's face. My dad has written a poem, which is beautiful, but is not read aloud. He leans on walls with the look of a person who endures.

After the casket is closed, there is a service in which there is a eulogy. My grandmother's brother talks about how my grandmother was a musician, how she loved to play the organ and the piano to accompany the services in church. I listen with more curiosity than reverence. I know that she had a piano, but I don't remember that I ever heard her play it. Is this where it came from? The music that runs in my family like blood?

At the graveyard, even my father seems to relax into the rhythm of articulate ceremony, or perhaps into the realization that the worst is past. His shoulders begin to release the weight. On the way back to the Salt Lake City airport, I tell him how I was touched by the realization that Grandma was the source of our family love of music, and how Nick and I have felt left out, but just the other day we decided to learn to play a song on the guitar. I chatter on about the broken guitar we got at the Goodwill, which is clearly worthless, but I hope that Jacob can at least give the thing a new set of strings.

My dad responds by offering me his own guitar. It hasn't been played, he says, in several years. He wouldn't miss it. At first I don't take this offer very seriously. Although we both are masters of talk, my father and I are not in the habit of relying on each other, even for small favors. But then he goes on to capture my heart in earnest. He tells me that his guitar has been pronounced dead by the coroner. He took it to be repaired and the shop said it was beyond repair, at which point he took it home and glued it up himself. My dad's guitar is reclaimed trash. It's treasure.

I promise to come again to his apartment the next time I'm in Boise and pick it up. I think I actually mean that, though one can never be absolutely sure. I get on my plane again humming "Froggy Went a Courtin'." And as we lift away from the sharp peaked mountains, I travel through early childhood memories, of cribbage games and song and open sky.

When I get off the plane again at Logan International, it is the middle of the night, and Nick and I fail to meet each other. I thought we said the fourth level of the parking garage, level with the sky bridge . . . but I don't see him. I am on foot and he is in a car and we do not have cell phones. We have simply missed each other in the thickness of a city airport, amid the layers upon layers of cars waiting like husks for their owner souls to come and reinhabit them. I take a cab home, knowing full well that Nick is wandering the airport, probably worried and definitely guilty, with two sleepy, grumpy children. I have no way to reach him. I may prefer my life without technology, but the interface between me and the rest of the world is a black hole into which my family has temporarily fallen.

I get home first, to a dark and empty house. When Nick comes in with the children, we don't fight and we don't apologize. He reaches out to me, caring, in the silent way he does, with the work of his hands. He gets the kids and all my things to rest before he looks at me expectantly and waits for me to talk.

I don't have many words left myself. "It was all right. Everything was all right. I'm glad I went."

He nods. We lie down together in the dark, in our bed that used to belong to Lady Macbeth, in our apartment two thousand miles away from where we came from. I can't help but think of my grandma's last words to me. She said, "It was nice to meet you."

I reply to her, through the long, wide dark from Boston to the Rockies. "It was nice to meet you too, Grandma. I'm glad you stopped by."

We drive down to New York to deliver to Dan one of Grandma's Bibles. Our grandmother didn't have much, but what she had we have tried to distribute. Dan takes the Bible and at the same time gives me a copy of his self-published guitar instruction book, *Guitar for Absolute Beginners*. It's just released. It's beautiful and funny, and I laugh at how great the timing is. Maybe Jacob can get the strings fixed on that broken guitar, and then I'll learn from this book. I tell Dan about number eight on our list, that Nick and I have decided that by this time next year we are going to be able to play a song on the guitar. He smiles at me encouragingly. He is another teacher, like Dolly, like Jacob, and like our mother. He says, "That is doable. That is definitely doable."

We haven't given Dan and Miriam any notice that we're coming, and as is often the case in the busy whirl of their lives, we are not the only dinner guests. As quick as can be, I'm getting to know this fun, accomplished couple that I've never met before and their three fun, accomplished kids. When the living room clears, I turn to Nick in utter disbelief. Is this what life is like for other people? Is this what it's like to live without perfectionism and performance anxiety? You just play Pictionary Jr. for a while and then head on out into the backyard to play some soccer? I am stunned by the gentleness of the world.

Dan and Miriam try to coax us to stay the night, but we have to drive home because I am scheduled to be the liturgist in church. The next day, I stand up at the lectern and lead the congregation in prayer. I expect the butterflies and the shaking hands, and I'm all ready to fight the good fight and get through it anyway, but they don't come. The fear doesn't come. I try to explain this later on the phone to Sara, my sister, and all I can think of to say is, "It's the whole thing. It's just the whole Year Without Internet thing."

Then I say a bunch of other stuff, but I feel myself turning into my *blah-blah-blah* self, the one that talks and doesn't say anything. I keep talking about conquering fear and conquering ego and how these two things are the same thing. I'm sounding a little like Yoda, like it's a great mystery, or a bridge you cross over a river as wide as the one that opened up between me and Jacob. But I don't actually believe that. I do think that this is the path less traveled, but I don't think that's because it's hard to find.

Healing is possible. And what's more, the guideposts on your personal journey toward healing are all right there for the taking. But they only show themselves when you've left the path to fame and glory, and even self-importance. These gifts only show themselves to a humble heart.

It is late September when Amy finally gets around to sending me all the letters I've written to her. There are a lot of letters. We've been writing so much to each other for almost a year.

The flat-rate envelope she used is an excavated urn of my own writing. I start to scan for topics, themes, nice collections of cleverness. First I begin to admire myself, then judge myself, then reconstruct myself. As if I had never broken the habit, I start to move the pieces around, again, like the puppet master of my life. How do I look in this moment? How do I look in this thought? How do I position these moments to look like the person I think I want to be?

I fold the letters again. I put them back in their envelopes. I close the package and take it back to the post office and mail it back to California. I explain to Amy that I have changed my mind. I thought I wanted all those details back. I thought I wanted the record of every moment so I could look at myself, so I could hold on to all these bits and pieces of time with both hands. But I was wrong. When my computer was stolen, the last electronic record of my life was taken away. I am trying to learn to receive that gift. I am trying to learn to recognize myself from the inside out, instead of in all these mirrors. I am trying to learn to feel this—myself, free.

When Jacob comes over for dinner on Thursday, he starts right away to change the strings on the broken guitar. But he has hardly begun when he shakes his head and hands it back to me. This guitar is too broken. The pegs are completely broken off. He can't fix it. I try to smile and say I don't care, but my cover isn't as good as it used to be. The truth is, I had already planned what song I was going to learn first, and Nick and I were excited to learn together, and Jacob knows it. I put the guitar down on the floor and tell Milo he can do whatever he wants with it. He turns it into the ladder of an imaginary fire truck.

My gloom doesn't last. We have a simple dinner of brown rice and our own homemade cheese and vegetables from the farmers' market, and Jacob enjoys it as much as he enjoys any of our dinners, possibly because he has a great gift for enjoying things. After dinner I give Jacob a ride home, and on the way I find myself telling him what I didn't quite tell Sara. I tell him that I think my performance anxiety is lifting because I have stopped tracking my life in a way that is intended to be public. I think I suddenly feel more relaxed because I just stopped trying to live every moment of my life worthy to satisfy an audience.

I don't know what possesses me to keep telling my brother things like this. It seems so likely that he will disagree with me that he will miss the point or over-intellectualize my feelings the way he does. But I keep talking anyway.

As we cross the Longfellow Bridge, I tell Jacob that I have always had an audience, ever since I was little and I was a supporting character in Mom's sideshow, and after that when I was such a freak in school because I was so young and poorly socialized and so likely to be talking about something weird and intense, like the senior project in which I used the overhead projector to display diagrams of different kinds of female genital mutilation. It was so obvious that I should make my career in alternative, low-budget theater. It was so obvious that I should write blogs about my life and relentlessly produce my self-awareness and post my feelings ad infinitum on the Internet. It was obvious that I should keep doing the thing that I have never learned how not to do, which is to perform.

Never in my life have I felt such total anonymity as I do right now. Never in my life have I stood so far from the portal that frames the stage. I used to think that it would be like dying. But it isn't like dying. It's much more like having a quiet place to rest.

I square my shoulders and prepare for my brother to tell me that I'm making things up. But he doesn't. Instead he looks out at the Charles River and the falling, creeping cold and says, "Yeah."

Then my brother tells me something he hasn't quite told me before. He says that he feels a pressure equally as intense. He feels a need to intellectually absorb all the knowledge in the universe. He says that it makes him uncomfortable to think that there are things out there that can be known that he doesn't know. He is driven to know all those things. Even though—he grimaces—that obviously isn't possible.

I don't make a single joke to Jacob about how I didn't realize that all this time he was actually trying to be a know-it-all on purpose.

All I say is "Wow," and then I say good-night and drive home. On the way I think about what it would have been like to be the one who knows stuff. I used to think Jacob was so lucky to be a college professor, to have something to contribute to nearly every conversation, and to have people think that he literally does know everything because he so often is able to say yes when someone says, "Have you read such-and-such?" He can speak with intelligence about so many things.

I have valued Jacob's immersion in the information stream for the same reasons I have valued my own. Like the rest of the Net Generation, I am driven by the fear of missing out. It is so easy to see in others—or imagine I see in others—a comparative closeness to the information source. Jacob has always been an example of this. He has always been in a coveted and desirable position because his library in books and brain cells is so vast.

Now his status as informed citizen seems no different than any other self-made prison, by which we limit ourselves to the things we think we need to be. He is lucky to be driven to achieve because he will achieve, and the world will reward him for it. But his achievement comes at a price. Achievement always does.

Now I think that maybe I'm the lucky one who was just a little bit behind in the matter of intelligence, partly because I'm younger, but also because I was pulled the other way, fiercely and constantly pulled back into the place of unknowing, back to the place where nobody gets to say that they're right because nobody is. I now know what hand has been pulling me, always, to let go and accept the path of peace. And I am humbled and amazed again by the sheer length of God's arm. I am amazed at the way that Love has come for me.

I don't want to tell my husband that I've been waiting for my brother's approval. But I have been. As angry as I might have been at my brother, he is the first man I ever loved, the man that pop psychology says is supposed to be your father. My brother's eyes make things real, and now this bizarre reshaping of the world is becoming real.

There is no public story of my life. There is no blog. I have no audience. There is no shadowy figure in the plush red seats to whom I am expected to deliver the sweet and funny details of my life in clever packaging. There is only empty space.

And in it . . . I am free.

Now it is my turn to reflect the sky, which has been all this time my teacher. I let the fears and the joys rain down and fall away. I cry at everything, all day long, in short spurts, and over the most ridiculous things. I'm taking my little kids for a walk along the beach. A policeman stops the traffic to help us cross the street, and I start crying. Because you know what? That is exactly how things are supposed to work. I take the kids to the grocery store, and a Down Syndrome parking lot attendant introduces himself to Milo, and Milo very seriously takes his hand and nods, and I cry because that too is just exactly how things are supposed to work.

I don't cry for only good things. I cry for Central America and our whole history of imperialism. I cry for Haiti. I cry for Nicaragua. I cry for all the small and far away countries that I can't call by name because, unlike my big brother, I'm not very good at remembering things like that. I cry too for my grandmother, and the ice in the air between her and my chameleon, insubstantial father, her son. And I cry for my mother and for my husband's mother.

While Stella naps, I sit in the chair in the kitchen and cry all afternoon for something deep and impossible to articulate. Milo is very concerned about me. He says, "Are you okay, Mama? Are you okay?" I reassure him that yes, I am okay, but I'm also not done crying, so he might as well go ahead and take the entire candy jar with him into the living room.

I am crying for the birth of all our stories, the myths that give life to the tigers we chase, our identities we form and reform, the scripts in which we play out our struggle for approval. I am crying because all those stories didn't have to be true. Jacob didn't have to be the smart one. I didn't have to be the drama queen. It just didn't ever have to be that way.

I understand now that I can still make records of my life. I can still write. I can still take pictures and caption them. Sometimes I will be thoughtful, or clever, and when I'm very lucky, I will make my girlfriends laugh. But I can never again record these words or pictures and call them the true measurement of my life.

The silence is a canvas that doesn't hold color. I can paint it however I want, and that's okay, but I have to understand that none of my colors will stick. This is how it happens that I am pretty much the same person, even though I have been going through transformations like hemorrhages. This is how it happens that every person I know sees my project differently, and some insist that it's going differently from how I think it's going. One person thinks I've been saved; another thinks I'm just barely going to make it; my kids don't see anything different at all; Nick sees me humming in the kitchen and says, "Look at you. You're so relaxed. It's beautiful."

My friend Missy's husband is an artist. Prolific. Intense. When I lived with them, briefly, after I left my husband, I watched him stay up all night in his studio, inking comic book covers, smoking cigarettes, and drawing, drawing, drawing. He admitted to me that it didn't always make sense, with a kid and a mortgage to pay and his wife not always crazy about the hours he keeps, but he said he keeps doing his art because he hasn't killed that tiger. He is chasing his tiger in color and ink, as Jacob is chasing his tiger in knowledge as, lately, I am chasing mine in tears. We're all just trying to be human.

I'm still a bit in a fog from all the crying when I go down to the basement to start a load of laundry, and there's a sock in my washer. It isn't my sock. It is a child's sock, but it is not one of my children's socks. I don't consider at all what I am doing before I pick up the sock and march directly up the stairs to knock on my upstairs neighbor's kitchen door.

"Is this your sock?"

"Yeah," she says. "I must have dropped it."

"No," I reply, "you didn't drop it. It was in my washer."

"It must have fallen in there."

"No. It was *inside* my washer. It was spun up onto *the side* of my washer. I think because you were using my washer to wash it." I don't leave any room for her to deny or confirm. I really, really don't care about the washer. I'm here for something that says, "Tell me, are you struggling?"

She tenses. "Maybe. A little."

"I'd like to help. How can I help?"

Instantly she starts crying. One hand reaches out over the baby gate, grasping at the air, as if looking for a shut-off valve. Her mouth is open, trying to get some words out. I want to turn around and run. I want to pretend this never happened. But I am struck to silence. How her tears are just like mine, how they hover in the air above us, how they separate and combine. How this is the thing that breaks down the distance between us—these tears we share.

Finally she gets the words out. Can I babysit? It's just her, to do everything, she says. Her son doesn't help out much anymore, and now that Tammi's gone . . .

She goes on, but I don't hear the next thing. I just hear the name. Tammi. *Tammi.* She has a name. The junkie, the thief, the dragon-wearer, the young mom, that troubled girl who lost a dog she loved. Her name is Tammi.

Can I babysit? You better believe I can babysit. Absolutely. Anytime, I'm always home, I never go anywhere. Now I'm trying to be funny. What else is there to do when your heart is getting pried open with a crowbar? I practically run down the stairs to start preparing. Tammi's son won't like our whole-grain food, won't be used to playing in a house without a television. I don't know any toddler other than Milo who spends quite so much time looking at books. But I'll change. It's worth it. I'll take them to the park. I know where the park is. I've always thought I ought to learn how to throw a ball. Maybe this is the moment when I will learn.

The next day my neighbor doesn't seem to remember our conversation. She doesn't need me to babysit that day, or the next day, or the next. I'm not sure if I dreamed up the whole thing. She still has that tough New England way about her. So I stop asking. But for months after, the memory of our meeting hangs in the stairwell. I take the steps down to the basement two at a time, running away from the intensity of it, this river of grief we share, the sadness that links us as close as sisters. No wonder we were such experts at not seeing one another. No wonder I used to close the drapes.

Twelve

Life for Absolute Beginners

It is October in New England. The fall in our beloved and maligned adopted home generously shows us its colors despite all the time we've spent complaining and trying to get back to where we came from. Nick and I drive down to New York to see our family and to watch the colors change along Merritt Parkway, the orange like a slow-motion fire spreading south. If we could see the way God sees, would even a forest fire move like this? Slow and steady, like a game of catch in the yard, the cycle of destruction and rebirth?

We come back into Boston and put on our coats and walk up in the Blue Hills. We climb what is called the Great Blue Hill, with Baby Stella in a backpack. At the top there is an observatory from which you can see the ocean and the city and a sign that notes with pride that this is the highest elevation in the United States along the Atlantic Coast—645 feet. We stand at the sign and laugh. We were born in the Rockies. We were born in wilderness. This record 645 feet is not an elevation that can impress.

But it is a beautiful walk. And it is made all the more poignant somehow by the nearness of the highway and the sound of airplanes overhead. Nick and I gather up discarded water bottles and potato-chip bags from around the observatory and put them in the trash bins. We pick up bottles and we try to live our lives without the Internet.

I know that we will leave this place. But for now we will stay. And I will practice complaining about the weather, the way people do in this part of the world. I will practice taking this constant abuse from the sky, as if it were a kind of dance with a wild God. And I will do my best to love this place. I will do my best to love this wind-swept ocean-low Atlantic coast, where the fire-colored trees and the wind and the seasons back you up against the wall of your mortality.

When my friends ask why we haven't moved West yet, we tell them it's all about the money. We've decided Nick will stay at this job three years so we can make it all the way out of debt. Our friends nod gravely. It seems so grown-up and plausible.

But truly, who can leave New England in October?

Nick takes a trip to Boise for Halloween and to offer companion-ship for a round of his mother's chemotherapy. He takes Milo with him in a homemade costume made to look like the green-spotted clown in *The Little Engine That Could.* I am left at home with Baby Stella. I immediately read four more books and then sit in front of the radiator and do the thing I have learned to call meditation. Then I practice my juggling.

I am singing along with Kenny Rogers on the record player when I first set a rhythm with three clubs. I'm howling, "*She believes in me . . . I'll never know just what she sees in me,*" when suddenly I discover that I am juggling three clubs, after dropping every time for literally hundreds of tries. I love this feeling. I love that this is possible. Growth is possible.

I catch myself wondering how on earth I'm going to explain this. How will I say this to the world? That I used to spend hours making mixes of the best and most current indie music to impress my friends, and now I sing along to a record I bought for twenty-five cents at a garage sale. Or that I used to do only things I knew I could be good at, and now I think nothing of spending an entire weekend learning a skill at which I will always be mediocre and which has little or no monetary value even when you're awesome. I don't have any idea how I can justify this. Not only this one moment, but all the things that have happened in this strange and strangely miraculous year of my life.

I feel the weight, then, that even miracles are temporary. The rubber band will snap back into its shape. Whether it is a blog, or a book, or just a conversation, I will be called out of my cave, this time not by the rhythm of the seasons, but by the mass of people from whom I have hidden my face. I will come out to meet that whole world of people and critics to whom I have so steadfastly refused to represent myself.

Already people ask how I'm feeling about it all. Am I glad the year is almost over? Do I want to go back on the Internet? I say, for God's sake, what a question. Of course I don't want to go back on the Internet. But I will. I will, I will, I will. Until then, please leave me alone. I have one more month. On November 1, I write down in my cornflower blue notebook, "Three clubs." Then I close the notebook and put it away. For this last month, I don't want to take any notes. I don't want to miss a single second of the silence and the rest. I know full well that I may be stocking up for the rest of my life.

I pick up Nick and Milo at the airport without parking and without problems despite our lack of cell phones or Internet. This is the rule. When you have tried to do something new that you didn't know how to do before, and you screwed it up X number of times, where X is some number between one (for caramelizing onions) and several hundred (for juggling clubs), you will then, the next time, get it right.

Milo is in a good mood from the airplanes and the visit. He chatters about wind and wings as Nick hands me a black guitar case. I don't look, but I know that inside is my dad's guitar. Jacob comes over right away and tunes it for me. He starts to play, and I join in with him on my living room floor, and together we sing:

> *Froggy went a courtin' and he did ride, uh huh, uh huh.*
> *Froggy went a courtin' and he did ride, uh huh, uh huh.*
> *Froggy went a courtin' and he did ride*
> *with sword and pistol by his side, uh huh, uh huh, uh huh.*

Jacob hands the guitar to me. He says, affectionately, "It's a great guitar."

I laugh so suddenly that I snort. Jacob laughs too. We look at the glue where Dad repaired the bridge himself. We look at the curve in the neck where the strings are lifting away from the fret board. It probably wasn't that great a guitar to begin with, about a hundred years ago.

"Well"—my brother tilts his head to the side the way he does— "you know what I mean."

"I do." I know exactly what he means.

Later, when I am mostly alone, I sit down with the guitar on my lap and open my oldest brother's guitar book, *Guitar for Absolute Beginners*, with the funny stories and the hand-drawn illustrations. I play the first chord, a D. It sounds terrible. I blow on my fingers and try again. It still sounds terrible. I feel fantastic.

I have found the one thing that I can always be good at. I can always be brilliant at this. I can always, no matter what, under any circumstances, be an absolute beginner. I might get it tattooed on my forehead.

A *few days later*, I'm on the phone with a creative friend, back in California, and I'm trying to explain to her how crazy it is what happened to my stage fright. I imagine that she will remember one particularly lurid event when I went onstage to fill in for an actor in my own production—Janet was in that show—and I literally shook the scenery with my nervous legs. I am explaining to her how that landscape has shifted, changed. And I tell her that I have been transformed by the resurrected Jesus Christ.

I can hear her intake of breath all the way across three thousand miles. She says, "You don't really believe that, do you?"

Too late I realize what an error I have made. I forgot that there are two languages. I just spoke in the wrong one. I spoke to my secular creative friend as if I were in a Christian church in Nicaragua. I try to take it back. I offer a secular translation, but it's too late. In the real world, when people talk like that, other people worry about them, and now Janet is worried about me. She says, "Esther, don't you know? People turn to things like this in times of trauma. And what you went through . . . leaving San Diego. That was trauma."

I am almost finished now with book number sixty-three, one that came from Nick's grandmother, in which a rabbi well versed in the "modern" psychology of fifty years ago is explaining that the mental disease of atheism can be triggered by experiences of trauma. I love the symmetry of this. Trauma: religion. Trauma: atheism. Hey, do you see that person who is different from me? The one with all the crazy talk about God? She is broken, not quite right inside. Backward, in fact. She has suffered trauma.

But, oh, isn't it the truth? Trauma shakes up the universe. It renames things. We come into a brokenness, and when we come out again, all the words are in a different order. Instead of pursuing intelligence and wisdom, as I was supposed to do, now I'm spending all my time down at the seashore, making cakes out of sand and blowing bubbles.

Hallelujah. Christ is risen. I am reborn.

I'm sitting at my desk, my heels curled up under me, reading something, when Nick comes around the corner and says, "I'm glad you're with me."

I say, "I'm glad you're with me too," and then he goes away. I flip some pages, but for some reason my book has become incredibly boring. I follow Nick into the kitchen, where he is making bread, and sit down to wait for him to talk. It takes a while. He puts the bread dough in a bowl, covers it with a cloth, and washes his hands. Then he begins to talk about his mother. He talks about her cough that she has had his entire life, and how he hates it now when anybody coughs. He talks about the fact that his mother smoked for forty-seven years before being diagnosed with the lung cancer that will kill her. He talks about how his brother, with the family trademark sharpness-masking-pain sense of humor, wrote on his Facebook status, after an update on his mother's fatal disease, "By the way, smoking is bad for you."

He leans on the counter. "Does he think she doesn't know that? Does he think she didn't know that the whole time?"

I nod, understandingly. I think I know what this is all about— why my generally silent, surly husband just out of nowhere told me that he's glad I'm around. He knows that I understand this thing about his mother. I understand it because I was once backed into that same corner, where smoking is self-care because you think it's the only thing you do for yourself and not for somebody else. It's the only thing you do that isn't what a good girl ought to do. And people tell you this one thing has to go. They tell you it's dangerous. They tell you it's selfish. In response you build a chain-link fence to protect yourself from those people who want to control you, who want to spread their guilt right into your lungs and take from you even that tiny postage stamp of personal territory.

But then, the aching part—oh, the aching part—is that you only want that fence for a season. Years later, or decades later, or maybe only a few minutes later, when your opposition backs down or gets distracted, you feel that you might want to change your mind, and you might try to crawl out through the chinks in the fence you made yourself.

I think that this is what Nick is talking about. But, as usual, I'm wrong. Now he begins to tell me another story. This one is about a bus ride with some young coworkers, and how he heard them talking about a person they knew who let go of a serious relationship and then regretted it, and how those young coworkers called that person stupid.

"They don't have any idea," Nick says. "They don't know what it is to have made that kind of mistake. And then to have to live with it."

My mouth opens and closes like a fish. I just figured out what we're talking about. We're talking about the time when my husband slept with my best friend on the night of our sixth wedding anniversary, when I was pregnant with our second child, and then, just for good measure, lied about it. He does know what it is to have made a mistake and then to have to live with it. And he knows that I have something more than compassion for this, because I have felt it too. "I know what it is to have made a terrible, soul-crushing mistake," Nick says, "and I still have you, and I'm grateful for that."

"I know," I say. "Me too."

There in the kitchen, we wind ourselves together into one thing and stand that way, with the rising bread, for a long time. We are united by choice. Not forced together by propriety, or obligation, or somebody else's family values, or even fear. We stand together by choice, with our massive, gaping failures, and our wounds, wrapped around each other like koala babies. And the silence comes in, and it gathers us together, and it fills in the cracks.

The healing isn't any more sudden than the breaking was. My spiritual life is like a walk across a canyon on a swinging bridge. To turn back is impossible. The bridge disappears. There is only forward. And all along the way, I can feel sorry for myself, and cry and moan because the ground is so far away and my path is so unsteady. If I want I can spend a half hour for every step, chewing on my fingernails and calling out for help that never comes. Or I can just keep walking. The bridge is already there, not somewhere out there on the distant horizon, and not delivered to my grasping hand, but already there, right underneath me, right under my feet.

I could, if I wanted, go back through my journals, and in every place that I have written the word "silence" I could cross it out and write "God." That's how it turned out. That's the truth of my faith. But it isn't how it came to me. The silence came to me as something bigger than my memories of Sunday school, wiser than our wars of conquest, and more precious than the territories on which we stake our claims. God came to me as the silence and the rest. God came as the place where we stop. And listen. And let go.

And my God is the Christian triune God, because I am a Christian. There has to be some place where you take refuge, and there comes a time when you find your refuge truly in that place. Christianity is the religion I was born into, and I was taught it, and when I close my eyes and see the world, it is Jesus who carries it on his bloody back. It doesn't help anything for me to pretend to be something other than what I am.

I am a Christian. But I am only one Christian. I am one person—digging in the sand by the sea for my share of meaning, and humility, and grace.

The hourglass runs out on December 1, 2010, at noon. The year is up. The morning is ordinary. We read books. We eat vegan chocolate cake for a snack. The quiet is like a breath. But then Stella goes down for her nap, and it is afternoon. I am about to turn on the old broken computer and click on the icon because, for goodness' sake, a year is a year and the year is up, when the phone rings.

It is an acquaintance, a friend of Jacob's, who has a daughter exactly the same age as Stella. Liz called because she remembered that I am about to go back on the Internet. She wants to know how it's been going and to congratulate me. She also wants to tell me that she has changed her mind about something. When she first heard me talk about the Internet as a destination—a place to which I travel—she disagreed with that. She said she could think of the Internet as a vehicle, or a tool, but not a destination.

At the time I was not a bit perturbed. Liz is a few years older than I am. I marked her down with the many, many others, like my father and my sister, who can use the Internet as a tool and not a country. But Liz recently moved to the other coast, to a new place where she lives in her new house with her young child and no job. Her voice thins slightly as she confesses that lately she has found herself often going to the Internet not for any particular reason but just to be there.

I murmur assent.

I don't ask Liz if she knows how precisely she is describing my own experience. But she must feel this, even over the phone. She must feel our deep connection. Because this is exactly what I have been talking about. This is the thing that happens to us. Maybe the move, maybe the departure, maybe some other expression of our freedom unravels threads knit loose to encompass other threads at greater distances. This is the condition of our families, divided from one another by great distances and expensive plane tickets, split at the core by long hours worked in divided worlds. This is our condition—the hours each day alone in our houses, or at our desks, more dependent on conveniences than on relationships, wondering why we feel such a deep craving to connect.

I tell Liz I'm glad she called. I understand. And I'm just about to go back on the Internet, so I'll post something on her Facebook page. She laughs and says good-bye. There is silence on the line.

I hesitate. Like the patriarchs in the book of Genesis, I build in this place a pile of stones to mark what has been, for me, holy ground. One stone for my husband. One for my brother. One for my friend, and one for my friend's little daughter, and one for mine. One for the career for which I once would have given anything, another for thinking God's face is more beautiful in a theater than in a kitchen. One big sharp rock for thinking my life would be better if only I were famous. And many pebbles for trying to run away from everything that hurts. It is a tower of tributes. I hope I trip over it every day. I hope it bangs my shins.

And then I'm on. On the computer, double click, jumping in. There are thousands of e-mails. Facebook postings. Tweets. I am having two IM conversations at the same time. I spend the whole afternoon drooling on my keyboard and pushing my children away. I don't sleep well. The next day I write a blog post about it. A few days later I write another one. My friends announce to one another that I have returned, and some people want to know how it all went. But I don't know how to tell anyone how it went, and I don't feel like posting blog posts every day. Within weeks the newness fades, and I have no habits of communication with which to replace it. I delete my Facebook page. I disconnect from 407 people. Some of them are sad. A few are hurt. Many don't really care. I just feel guilty.

Did Copernicus feel like this, I wonder, when he said to the Earth, "I don't believe you are the center of the universe"? Did he hurt the Earth's feelings? Did the Earth writhe and roll with more authority, trying to maintain its centrality against the press of scientific discovery? I don't know. But history moves only forward. The Earth does not recover its old position. Nor do I. I tell my friends to call me, but they don't. I tell them to write letters. They act as if I'm joking. I use e-mail, and before long I too fall out of the practice of writing letters.

I hold on by a thread—one foot in the world, one foot out. I am grumpy. The world reaches out with full hands—iPods and iPads and Pinterest pins—but I turn up my nose at the offerings. The present reality is pulling on me, calling me to be here and now, in 2010, in this millennial age. But I keep pushing back. I'm afraid that if I carry my transformed self back into my old places, the transformation will disappear like a puff of smoke. I'm afraid I'll find out nothing really happened after all. For weeks it goes like this. Reality pulls at me to come in all the way, and I resist.

But there is an answer to every cry. When I feel dead, I plant something. When I feel forgotten, I create something. When I feel unforgiven, I pick up the guitar. In the mornings I sit on a pillow with my legs crossed, facing the radiator. Some days my whole brain gets wet in the dew of the resurrection. Other days I feel annoyed and scratch my face. But I sit. I stay. I roll over. I give my belly to the time. And the silence touches me. God with his mighty hand wipes clean my brow.

There is an image in the book of Revelation—the youngest segment in what Thoreau calls a very old book and the place where I started my own backward-returning journey—in which the faithful are each gifted a white stone. It is symbolic of their spiritual rebirth—a white stone with one's new name.

This is the prize that I found, mostly by accident. After thirty-one years of fumbling my way around this apparatus, this human soul, without instructions, I finally bumped into the reset button. We have one. Can you imagine? I had no idea. The reset button, the do-over button, the "if only I had my life to live over again" button. It was there all along. But oh, what it costs your ego to keep on pressing it.

A church friend passes me a note one day after worship. On the back of a folded program insert he has scribbled an excerpt from a poem by Denise Levertov. He says, "I think you might find this helpful."

> *the wings of the morning*
> *brush through our blood,*
> *as cloud-shadows brush the land.*
> *What we desire travels with us.*

I stand in the near-empty cathedral, beneath the Tiffany windows backlit by daylight, and clutch the mint-green paper in my hand. *What we desire travels with us.* Ever since I first met the silence—way back in the falling snow, in my first Sabbath trance, on the day after my husband's thirty-third birthday—I have been looking for a way to make that feeling permanent. I've been looking for a way to make it stand still, but it can't stand still. It can't stand still because *I* can't stand still. I just have to believe this miracle truth—that God loves me enough to travel with me.

A year ago, I set out to go for a year without the Internet. It was an experiment, but I didn't know the variables. I didn't know that when I opened this much space and margin in my life to allow the silence to flood in, I would also awaken a powerful desire for spiritual experience. I didn't know how much hunger I was keeping numbed by speed and noise. But what I really didn't know was just how close to me was the answer to that ravenous longing.

It is worth it to go looking for redemption. It can be found. Healing is possible. Things *do* grow again. We underestimate our own tremendous capacity for recovery, the capacity of the organism to heal itself.

I know how easy it is to think your ugly is too ugly, your broken is too broken. But this is the whole sum of what I've learned. There is no wound too small or too horrible to be a candidate for healing, though that healing may require that you give up more than you ever dreamed. This is the length of God's arm.

Go to the silence. In the silence there is glue. And you may find there too that God is already traveling with you—too big to see, and too close to feel, but as unmoving and vast and generous as the sky.

Epilogue

We stuck it out in Boston for three years. It was three years to the day—and not a single minute more—when we traveled debt free back to the mountains and the piercing blue sky of Idaho. Once there we moved with our (now three) children into a yurt on a mountainside and launched an off-grid homesteading adventure. And so begins another story.

After my Year Without Internet, I launched myself quite fully back into the world of cyber connection. I blogged again, made videos, made online friends. When I picked up my screens again, I found them already buzzing with every single one of my new passions: organic gardens, DIY economics, whole foods, and homestead family values.

In the end, the last laugh was on me. Even at my most isolationist moment, when I struck out to walk where there is no path, I was accompanied by thousands of my closest friends. Just when I turned up my nose at the network and unfriended all my Facebook friends, right at that moment I was living in community.

Because this is what our generation is doing. We are busting out and breaking down, rearranging and reconstructing. We are carving out the stuff that doesn't work, and trying to gather the tools to build the things that do. We have no choice but to do this. This is the world we have inherited, and it is broken.

For three years, Nick and I lived in Boston, learning and studying and preparing to walk in my mother's footsteps toward a different kind of life. My son turned four and then five and started school, and my little baby daughter drew on the walls and became a small person. And then, in the late spring that was thick with lilac blossoms, my husband's mother died of lung cancer. We all went back to Idaho to sit with her and to show her that we had learned to play her favorite song on the guitar and to say good-bye. A few weeks after that, my husband's grandmother, my first real pen pal, died, and I took home another box full of her books.

And finally, that fall, under the orange leaves dying all around us, another woman's mother died, the elderly mother of my upstairs neighbor, Maggie.

I told Maggie to take good care of her heart, which is just something I say, and she leaned across the fence and gave me an unexpected, awkward, one-armed hug. That night I finally got to babysit her grandson, who ran like a wild thing around my house and taught my kids to play "Monstah" with a dropped "r," as if Dorchester were their very own natal shore. And when the little boy's mother—whose name is Tammi—came back from wherever the G-men took her, with no dragon hanging around her neck and some extra pounds and a couple of new tattoos, I walked right up to her and shook her hand. I told her I was glad she was back.

Is this possible? How is this possible? I have no idea. But beneath our presenting faces, we are all made of the same fleshy stuff. Isn't it a miracle?

I feel like I'm riding a wave. Everything I do and discover is happening at the same time for ten other people I don't know. Or more. Everything I write is being said at the same time by somebody else. There are so many people who want what I want—to live with more accountability, more honesty, and more self-reliance, to live closer to the land as well as the sky. I might not have ever realized this if I hadn't gone back on the Internet.

The Internet is different for me now because I am different to it. I tread carefully, knowing that I am like a crow that chases shiny things, and the Internet is one great wide ocean of shiny foil and foam. But I do go back. I know that it isn't really advertising revenue that drives the clinking, clanking Internet machine. It isn't really the false world either, or the greed, or the pretty mirrors in which we see our own reflections. It's us. I'm there. And you're there. And we go to see each other.

Hi.

Acknowledgments

S ome books are quick in the making, or so I've heard, but this one was slow. Years and years of relationships and human souls have contributed to the growing of it, from my seventh-grade English teacher right through to the people who watch my YouTube channel now. My heart is full.

To the team at Zondervan, seriously I don't know I got to be so lucky. Alicia, thank you. Jim, thank you. Stephanie, you're a genius. Time will tell. And for the time that I turned off track changes . . . let's just say you deserve a year without the Internet.

To my agent, Don Jacobson, thanks for taking me on. Blair Jacobson, thanks for encouraging my worst jokes and my best courage. Sarah Bessey and Seth Haines, thanks for being the kind of writers I wanted to become.

To all my Bible studies and Christian writers' groups, thank you for holding my nervous hand and intermittently quoting Romans 1:16. Abby, Tanya, Caris, Jamie B., and all the Inkwellians, thank you for getting me through so many stages of birth, especially transition. Sorry about the mess.

To everyone who let me tell your stories, thank you. To the lovely people of Church of the Covenant in Boston, especially

Stephanie, Polly, Emma, Tim, and Pastor Jennifer, thanks for being the beautiful house I blew through. And to Amy and Emily, and all the actors, designers, critics, and technicians of my theater years, thank you for being my adopted family.

Missy Bradstreet, I tried to shake you, the way I shook most everybody else, but your friendship held. Thank you for being my hope that not everything crumbles.

Jacob, you'll always be the one whose opinion mattered first. Thank you for letting me tell the truth about that dart in my leg. To my dad and all of my siblings, you're the most amazing people I've ever met. What a tribe to be born into!

And to my mother, who knew before I did what a terrible devastating sweetness it is to write a book, I'm sorry I didn't give you more credit earlier on. Thank you for coming back to help me when I needed you.

Several other people who should be reading these thank-yous right now aren't here to do so. Bernie, Rick, Newell, Kit, thank you for giving of yourselves to me and to this story. I am trying to forgive you for dying.

And finally, the most enduring and wordless and helpless thank you goes to my husband and children. Nick, Milo, Stella, Sadie . . . you're everything.